W0232683

PENGUIN BOOKS
INTRIGUES OF THE LION

Carl Muller (1935–) is an unusual man. He is no academic; kicked out of three schools, he never went to university and served in the Royal Ceylon Navy, the Ceylon Army and the Port of Colombo as a pilot station signalman. In advertising briefly, he was also involved in the travel trade, and donned the robes of an entertainer. A pianist and a journalist, Carl Muller has a large number of published titles, ranging from poetry to science fiction, under his belt. His 'Burgher novels' earned him special acclaim, especially the first one, *The Jam Fruit Tree*, which won the Gratiaen Memorial Prize, 1993, for the best work of English literature by a Sri Lankan. He has also won the State Literary Award for his historical novel, *Children of the Lion*, the first book in this series.

He lives with his wife, Sortain, in Kandy.

Intrigues of the Lion

CARL MULLER

PENGUIN BOOKS

An imprint of Penguin Random House

PENGUIN BOOKS

USA | Canada | UK | Ireland | Australia
New Zealand | India | South Africa | China | Singapore

Penguin Books is part of the Penguin Random House group of companies
whose addresses can be found at global.penguinrandomhouse.com

Published by Penguin Random House India Pvt. Ltd
4th Floor, Capital Tower 1, MG Road,
Gurugram 122 002, Haryana, India

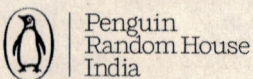

First published by Penguin Books India 2013

Copyright © S.O.R. Muller 2013

All rights reserved

10 9 8 7 6 5 4 3 2

ISBN 9780143414490

Typeset in Palatino by InoSoft Systems, Noida
Printed at Repro India Limited

This book is sold subject to the condition that it shall not, by way of trade
or otherwise, be lent, resold, hired out, or otherwise circulated without the
publisher's prior consent in any form of binding or cover other than that in
which it is published and without a similar condition including this condition
being imposed on the subsequent purchaser.

www.penguin.co.in

This is a legitimate digitally printed version of the book and therefore might not
have certain extra finishing on the cover.

'Individual existence as well as the whole world, are in reality nothing but a process of ever-changing phenomena which are all comprised in the five groups of existence. This process has gone on from time immemorial before one's birth, and also after one's death it will continue for endless periods of time. The five groups of existence are "Not Self" nor do they belong to a Self. The belief in any form of Self must be regarded as an illusion. All existence is void of a permanent self or substance...'

—The Anatta Doctrine of the Buddha
(Translated by Ven. Nyanatiloka Maha Thera in
The Path of Buddhism)

Contents

THE RIGHT TO LOVE

'Maiden stay! Do not descend. It is the viceroy of this land that bids you remain where you are.'

With a cry, Devi raised a trembling hand to her face, dropping the flowers she had picked. Even though they fell at Saliya's feet, he heeded them not, for his eyes were fixed on the girl, drinking in her incredible beauty. He stepped back, a sandal crushing an Asoka flower. He could play the prince well enough, he thought. Of a certain, she knew who he was but her eyes were pools of fear. He saw the way her knees shook and for a moment he feared for her, thinking she may fall. He wanted her to remain where she was. Her ragged cloth did little to hide her form, full-fleshed and golden, and he saw the way her breasts arched as the slender arm curved to bend at the elbow, tapering fingers spread across her face. He saw the way her hair stirred, and he felt his spirit reach up as if to enfold her.

'So lovely a maid, and yet do you forget yourself and climb like a playful boy? Will you come down now, and do you need my help?'

Slowly, the girl reached out to a branch and her face crimsoned. 'Forgive me, great prince,' she said, 'but I knew not that there would be anyone to see me.'

Saliya smiled. 'Fear not, for none else do. None save I, and I have watched you pick the Asoka flowers before. Will you come down?'

Devi looked down. She knew that the prince watched her every move; knew that he had seen her as no man ever had. She had to stoop, bend her knees, reach for the lower branch with her toes; knew that her scant cloth would hide nothing from the man below. Why did he not turn away? Why did he stand there, watching her every movement? She bent, then straightened herself, tugging her cloth about her knees.

'Shall I come to you, help you down?'

She shook her head in alarm. 'I can come down, great one, only...'

Saliya refused to consider the plea in her voice. 'Well, hurry then, for you keep your prince waiting. I have much to say to you.'

With a sharp breath, Devi inched down, her cloth sliding up her thighs as she arched her feet for footholds on the lower branches. Saliya watched. A heavenly maiden, he thought, coming down to snare the senses of man. She had her face to the mottled trunk when her feet touched the grass and she stood, turned away from him, adjusting her cloth, smoothing it down her sides.

Saliya went to her, turned her to him, led her to the shelter of a rock. 'You have dropped your flowers,' he said gently, 'but do not be sad. If it is your wish, I will pick more for you. Can I not climb higher than you?'

She was like a frightened doe. He saw how the blush remained on her face, and yet her lips quivered. His hand was firm at her elbow. 'Sit,' he said, 'and do not be afraid. See, I will sit too, by your side, and do you know why, my beautiful one? Because you have me at a disadvantage.

Yes,' he smiled, 'for even as you know who I am, I know not who you are.'

She looked up at him. 'I...I...I cannot remain like this, lord—it is not—not fitting. I...I am...'

'Stay. Have I not told you that I have watched you before? Aye, you come from the Helloli village, do you not? I have followed you to the bounds of the chandala encampment. So I know something of you—that you are of Helloli; and I know of your father too. The chief of the chandala, is he not? Stay. It pleases me that you sit beside me. I want you beside me always. Do you see there, near those trees? My horse stands there. Walk with me...come.'

He took her hands, raised her up. She did not try to take her hands away. With lowered head she said, 'Great lord, you but amuse yourself, but if it pleases you, I will walk with you.'

'And you will ride with me...and have no fear, maiden, for none frequent the paths we take.'

A nameless fear gripped Devi. How had she dreamed of this prince, spoken his name to herself. How she loved him...and yet, would he take her away on his horse...take her where? Would he heap abuse on her love, use her in some patch of the woods, drive her home with gifts and coin? What else would a prince wish of a chandala girl? Her fear rose with each step she took. What had her mother said? Yes, she was of that age. She needed a husband. A husband would be found her...

Saliya placed a hand on her hip. 'Who are you? Tell me of yourself, for this have I burned to know since the day I first saw you.' They stood beside the horse.

'I am called Devi, lord. I live the lowly life of the chandala and am shunned in the city because I am an outcast. This is why I come to the Asoka grove when my morning's work is done, for the flowers are beautiful and each tree is a king who wears scarlet crowns. I pick the flowers and make garlands for myself, for I may not cover my body, being but the lowest of the city dwellers.'

Saliya traced a finger down her cheek. 'You are as a goddess from the skies, my beautiful one, and with me will you remain. In all the land I have never seen one that equals you. Do you not believe me? Look into my eyes and see your face reflected there and know I speak true.'

'I—I am but a poor creature, great lord. No treasures have I. I adorn myself with the Asoka flowers. My cloth is ragged and grown short, for this have I washed and worn for many months. Do not mock my poverty, lord.'

Saliya smiled. 'Poverty, you say? Do you know that without thee I will be the poorest in all the world? See you, my beautiful Devi, often are precious gems, pearls, treasures cast away because they have fallen into dung. You are such a treasure, and though you be a chandala, you are my most precious treasure. What say you now?'

'But, lord...'

'But we shall ride. Let me help you mount. Do not be afraid. Yes, swing your leg over. What? Have I not seen you descend the tree? What secret can you hide from me now? Good...now move yourself up, forward, that I may find room to sit too.'

Devi stiffened, then relaxed. A warmth swept through her as she felt him behind her, his arms encircling her as he took up the reins. His thighs hugged hers closely and she felt the press of his body against her as he gave a small twitch of the reins, made a soft clicking sound. She knew his face lay against her head and that her shoulders touched his breast. She gave a soft gasp as the horse began to move.

'Lean back into me and you will ride with ease,' he said. 'Are you happy to ride with me?'

Carl Muller

What could she say? This could not be real. She should be going home, to the little hut in the compound where the water pots waited to be filled, where her mother sat grumbling to herself as she de-stoned the rice. There was the bandicoot trap at the edge of the fence and her father would be by the river, seeking the big water rats in the marshy grass. And where was the prince taking her?

'I have heard you sing. Your voice is as sweet as the bells that ring in the mountain temples. Will you sing for me?'

Somehow, she had snuggled into him and never wanted the ride to end. 'Where do you go, my lord?'

'We skirt the rice fields and the tall *timbiri*[1] and beyond lies the Issarama temple. There do we go, my love, and there will I ask of thee a boon...no, let me finish what I wish to say, for surely will you say that you have nothing to give. But you have. You will give me that most precious thing we all seek. You can give me happiness, for I have not rested since the day I first saw you. Even as I rode the city as viceroy, even as I led the escorts that accompanied the queen on her journey south, I searched among the faces of the chandala quarter, and I did not see you. Did you not join the throngs at the barriers?'

Devi's blood pounded. What could she say? That she had stood among the crowd, that her heart had ached for him even as he rode proudly by. She felt his arm encircle her, knew that her breasts lay upon his forearm.

'You will be my princess, my dearest, for none will share my life save you,' he murmured.

She closed her eyes, allowed the magic to surround her. What was it? The magic of his nearness, his arms around her, his legs pressed against hers, his breast heaving against her back. Her hand crept up, her fingers touching his arm. 'I will give you your happiness, lord,' she whispered, 'but how can I remain at your side? The people will be angered...your father will be angered...'

'What care I? I will not countenance their disapproval. They shall see how rare a treasure I have found.'

They did not stop at the stones before the temple but took the path beside the pool of dark water. A man stood there, and Saliya frowned, then allowed himself a small smile. He brought the horse to a halt.

'Go you to the cave of the ascetics, my lord?'

Saliya nodded. 'We see no more of your art, elephant-carver. Is it that you still wait to make the tablet you told us of?'

'That I do, lord, that I do. Perhaps the time of waiting is over?'

'Perhaps...but impose not on us, elephant-carver. You are man of many visions. We go to seek our own vision.'

'As I said you would, lord.'

'Yes, elephant-carver, and you have our gratitude. Is this not a far better thing we do?'

'It is what befits a man, lord. When we last spoke there was but the beauty of the man unmade; but now I see that there is a man, and such a man will I immortalize.'

Saliya nodded. He was not uneasy in the presence of the sculptor who had lain with him in the cave. He felt neither guilt nor shame. They had loved in that strange quickening way that he had known of so well. A boy then, a man now, and he would love this girl as befits a man. 'Mark us well, O carver of the elephant. Dwell upon the lines of form and face. When you carve, leave none of the grace untouched. Let your chisel proclaim old love and new and see to it that we smile, for now comes knowledge from the lessons of dalliance past.'

The man bowed. His grey eyes seemed to rake the pair on the horse and his lean fingers moved as if he was imprinting the form upon the mists of his artist's soul. Saliya touched the reins.

'See that we are not disturbed,' he said. 'For your tablet I will reward you with much coin and a land where you may live all your days.'

They cantered away. At the cave, he helped her off the horse. 'You are mine,' he said simply.

Her lips parted. She looked into his face and knew that she would give herself gladly. 'Am I truly yours, lord?' she whispered.

He took her hand. 'Come. In this cave none will dare disturb us.'

It may be said that Saliya and Devi gave themselves to the 'right to love' for it is evident that the society of the times deemed love and the joys of love to be the highest of all earthly blessings. We see that even in ancient India, the five sons of Pandu pondered on this: Which is the highest—dhamma, artha or karma? Religion, prestige or love? Many passages teach that love is the highest thing[2] and it is this that impelled Saliya and Devi to turn to each other. The *Book of Manu* is very decided about love. As it says:

> Now love itself springs from *sampalkat*[3] and *harsha*[4] is born of this sampalkat, and is born from sound, and is born, too, from taste, and is born, too, from form, and is born, too, from the touch, and is born, too, from the smell.

Whatever forces brought Saliya and Devi together, it was certain that the union would cause much dissension in the kingdom. Could Devi be Saliya's wife? We read in the Mahabharata that formerly

> ...women were unconfined and roved about at their pleasure, independent. Though in their youthful innocence they went astray from their husbands, they were guilty of no offence.

The custom of marriage was regulated by Swetaketa, son of the Raihi Uddalaka.[5] In old Ceylon, even the Veddahs, according to Tennent[6]

> ...acknowledge the marital obligations and the duty of supporting their own families.

Saliya knew that in choosing an outcast girl he would have to admit to a durable connection that must last beyond the mere act of propagation—weaving marriage and family together. It was not merely a giving of self to each other but the bonding of a common future, come what may. He knew full well, and so did Devi, that their 'happiness' would soon be 'arranged'. There was something unnatural about celibacy, and as Davy tells us, among the Sinhalese are hardly any old bachelors and old maids. He also goes on to say that when a young man has reached the age of eighteen or twenty, it is the duty of his father to provide him with a proper wife.[7]

The ancient nations of Aryan stock regarded celibacy as both an impiety and a misfortune.[8] The *Brahmadharma*[9] declares that until he finds a wife, a man is only half of a whole.

All women too, without exception, were obliged to marry. To Devi's mother, her daughter was of 'that age', ripe for marriage. The problem was that the Buddhist doctrine

Carl Muller

would have frowned upon the union of a prince and a chandala maid. Saliya knew how his teacher monks held lust and ignorance as the two great causes of the misery of life. The monks went farther. In the *Dhammikasutta*[10] it is declared that a wise man should avoid married life as if it were a burning pit of live coals.

Even Rhys Davids said that sensuality was simply not compatible with wisdom and holiness, and that is why the Buddha's mother had no other sons and that her conception was due to supernatural causes.[11]

Another hurdle, as Saliya knew, was whether in taking Devi, he would be placing himself and the chandala girl in the position of having contracted a 'blameable marriage'. There were, in those times, 'blessed marriages' in which the father gives away his daughter and from the union springs forth upright sons. But there were also four 'blameable marriages'—those effected by purchase, voluntary union, forcible abduction and stealth—from which, as was believed, sprang cruel and untruthful children.

Even as Saliya spent himself in Devi's arms, he knew the wonder of taking his first woman; even as Devi cried out at the taking of her virginity and he felt the warm touch of her blood that clung to the bottom of her vagina, they both knew that there would be the greatest opposition to their plans to live as one.

Marriage. There is, of course, the 'love marriage'. To this day, as it was in ancient times, if the couple in love belonged to the same caste, and if there were no other serious obstacles, parents would give their sanction and their blessings. And yet, such marriages are the exception.

More often than not, an intermediary is needed to find the right partner for a son or daughter. As Ratnapala says: 'The institution of the *magul kapuwa* or the marriage broker arose to answer this socio-cultural need.'[12]

Prince Saliya knew that he would be arousing a hornets' nest. What obligations could he fulfil? There was, at first instance, the dowry—one of the most important aspects and of ceremonial signifance.[13] Again, there would arise matters of social status, caste, and the reading of the horoscopes. The suitability of caste is rigidly upheld. Horoscopes too must be compared and found compatible. In earlier days, there was no hard and fast rule for the publication of banns. Village life was more intimate and the people, even in as large a city as Anuradhapura, knew each other. However, the statement of the auspicious times for the performance of the various ceremonies—the *Nekatpata*—needed to be prepared. This statement gave details of the couple, their parents, status and caste.

Devi watched her prince as he stood at the mouth of the shelter. She knew he was troubled and she did not wish to disturb his thoughts. They had lain on an old deerskin that was so worn that it crumbled at the touch. Perhaps it had belonged to some ascetic of old who had tenanted this cave. She moved her legs, saw the stain of red on the pelt. With a small sigh, she sat up, began to tear round the stained area with her fingernails.

Saliya came to sit beside her. 'What is it you do?' he asked.

'It is not right to leave this as it is,' she said. 'It is *kili*,[14] is it not?'

He nodded. Always there was the impurity that was connected with the flow of blood. Devi would carry away the piece of deerskin, put it in some place of purification. 'Are these the customs of the chandala as well?'

'Yes, my lord, and it is necessary for your protection. If the blood is permitted to remain, surely it will turn to water, and we shall die.'

Saliya pulled her to him gently. 'I will take this piece of skin, keep it with me. No demon will come as long as I hold it close.'[15]

'No, my lord. This must I keep until I bathe on the third day, and I may not help my mother cut the reeds for the making of mats until then. She will ask why, and what can I say to her...'

Saliya stroked her hair. 'You are so beautiful,' he murmured. 'Did I hurt you much?'

Her hand crept around his waist. 'You are my god. I used to stand beneath the Asoka trees and sing my love for you, and on my mat at night I would see you in the shadows. But I am so foolish an outcast. Will you bring me a white cloth that I may wear after I bathe? It is necessary that I wear white, so that the kili goes away and threatens us no more.'

Nodding, he took her by the shoulders. 'I know not what you must do and know but a little about this kili, but I do know that you cannot go back to your mother. What will happen when you do? Do you wish that I place the white cloth under the Asoka tree? And will not there be questions—and will not your people be seeking you even now? No! What am I if I must keep you a secret and come to you as a thief? What will you tell your mother? That you have lain with the prince? They will flee the city, carry you away. No! You will return with me to the palace and there will I say to all that you are mine!'

Devi gave a small cry. 'But lord...my lord, what think you the king would say...and the ministers—and the people, and...and...'

'Hush, we have each other. You are my Devi, my Asoka Mala Devi…my wife of the Asoka flower garland, and so will you be mine for all time. None shall stand between us!'

Many hours later they rode back. Saliya sat, proud in the saddle, and Devi sat side-saddle for the soreness of their lovemaking made her cry out when she tried to mount.

'Do not be afraid,' he said, 'and heed not the stares of the people, for we will ride through the Eastern Gate that all may look upon us. Your parents too. We ride as one, my beloved, for one we are, come what may.'

From the rocks the elephant-carver watched them go. The boy he had loved, the boy who had lain naked, pulsing in his arms, was now a man. No longer would the prince seek the love of men. There, in front of him, sat the woman of his choice. He had put away the loves and dalliances of his youth for the natural love of a woman of divine beauty.

He watched them take the road to the city. Now he would set to work. What a tablet of stone would he carve.

A MIRACLE IN THE MAKING

It is 135 BC. DUTTHA GAMANI HAD AGED. HE HAD NEVER REALLY regained himself after the passing away of his mother and for many moons he lay as though he would will the world to stop turning, seeking to bring back the days of his sensational campaign, his vengeful march on Anuradhapura. He would talk all the time of the days that were, the days when his mother rode with him, a flaming figure of indomitable will. It was his brother, Saddha Tissa, who watched over him, urging him to look ahead, insisting that the king go out in his palanquin each day to see how the marvel of the Maha Thupa fared. Duttha Gamani would gaze up and around, and there would be a hint of desperation in his voice. 'Will it be finished?' he would ask. 'It must be finished. We cannot die lest it be finished.'

Saddha Tissa would grasp his brother's hand. 'It will be. It will. It is a stupendous work and indeed a miracle. Your miracle, my brother.'

A miracle indeed, for Saddha Tissa knew how much the colossus was costing and how many toiled to raise it. The bubble shape—the *bubulakara*—of the stupa was now beginning to gleam like warm milk in the sun as the plaster was laid on…and yet, there was so much to do. The three *malakas*[16] had been completed. There was yet the superstructure to be attended to, the wall of elephant heads to be built. It was fortunate, he thought, that a rich vein of silver had been found at Ridigama. It helped to cover expenses. Already, the officers of the treasury said 6,400,000 coins had been paid in wages, and there was no way he could counter his brother's orders that no one should work without wages. At the outset, Duttha Gamani had arranged for 1,600,000 *kahapanas*,[17] garments, ornaments, soft and hard food, beverages, perfumes, garlands, molasses, oil, clay vessels and a variety of other things in heaping quantity to be made available. 'Let one work as one desires and take of what I offer as one desires,' he had said.

The work following the long wait for the settling of the foundation, the knitting of the crushed stones and butter clay, the laying of the quartz and iron, the resin of the wood-apple mixed with mercury, the setting of the silver and bronze and the layering of arsenic and sesame oil had progressed rapidly enough, and even now the relic chamber was being completed beside the central platform as was the chattra to crown the stupa.

Saddha Tissa was worried. He knew that a miracle was in the making, but he also knew that just as a pot that is watched seemingly never boils, the work seemed to drag on. Other things also added to his worries. The wise men had wished him to be his brother's successor, but Duttha Gamani had shown, in one way or another, the need to school the prince Saliya to be king. That was really of no concern. He wished to return to Ruhuna for he feared for the peace of his kingdom where his sons, hotheads as they were, could not be relied on to share their royal duties.

Why did his mother have to die...and was she really dead? The strange manner of her passing worried him.

Carl Muller

Had she simply withdrawn, thinking perhaps that there was little need of her presence in a land secured for the Sihala and the Dhamma for all time? He walked alongside the palanquin, pointing out to his brother the progress made. 'It will be finished soon,' he assured, 'very soon.'

'But the railing? Where is the railing? Of gold it must be...and did I not say that the upper part of it must be of lacquered wood and gold...is it being wrought?'

'It is, brother. It will be installed soon.'

'Eighteen years has it taken. We must make a ceremony, brother. Let the monks know of our wishes that we call on the grace of the four Buddhas who have rendered this site sacred.'[18]

'That will we do. Is it that you wish the aid of the Blessed Ones to hurry the completion?'

'Yes, yes, it *must* be completed. We will beseech all the deities. It must be completed.'

Tissa knew that the adornment of the relic chamber would take time. In other dagabas, relic chambers were small. At the Thuparama, the repository was only as deep as the knee, and built at the summit of the dome. Here it had to be very much larger and placed low down the building. But he could not but marvel at all that had been so far achieved. 'O king, my brother,' he said huskily. 'What has been done has no man done before. You have given to the land a true marvel. But now the sun grows hot. We shall return.'

'No, let us remain. We wish to walk the terraces, see that all goes as we have wished. Do you think that to carry me here, carry me away, satisfies me? Let the bearers rest while we make inspection.'

How long ago, Duttha Gamani thought, that the drums had summoned the brick-makers and masons. Five hundred had assembled. 'How will you do this work?' he had asked and one had replied that with one hundred workmen he would use a cartload of earth each day. Others said they could do it with half as much—two *amana*s.[19] Duttha Gamani was not satisfied. Too much earth was needed and the laterite for brick-making was found some ten miles from the city. It would take time for the ox carts to carry all the laterite needed. He knew that a stupa as immense as he wished this to be would exert tremendous pressure on the foundation. Ordinarily, mortar would surely crack. Each brick needed a coating of laterite slurry to create a tight bonding. What he wanted was that the foundation become not just a quantity of laid bricks but, bonded together, become as a single enormous brick. He was pleased with the mason who proposed pounding the laterite in mortars and grinding what fell from the sieves, using but one amana a day. 'It is well,' he had said, 'but when the stupa begins to rise, it must rise faster than the grass will grow.' Yes, he had been pleased—so pleased that he had given the mason a pair of rich garments, ornamented shoes and 12,000 pieces of coin. So much had happened. He thought of the day he had laid the festival brick—of the pomp and ceremony. The *Mahavamsa* tells of his proclamation:

> Reverend lords, initiative of the construction of the Great Cetiya! I shall tomorrow lay the festival brick of the edifice. Let all the priesthood assemble there. Let all my pious subjects, provided with Buddhistical offerings and bringing fragrant flowers and other oblations, repair tomorrow to the site of the Maha Thupa.

He had commanded that the site, the road leading to it, the whole city be decorated. At the four gates were provided baths, barbers, clothing and garlands of flowers and provisions for the people. What a proud day that was. He had gone, attired in his robes, attended by his ministers, surrounded by a throng of dancing and singing girls. Forty thousand followed and there were full bands of musicians. At the site he had made a large offering of cloths and garments to the people and taken his place in the centre of the holy spot, surrounded by the monks. To each monk he had bowed, offered a fragrant garland, then had gone to the centre of the site where a minister awaited with a silver compass.[20]

It had been a matter of form to turn the tracer arm for there were many who gave willing help, and the circle was finally described. That first brick—what a joy it had been to lay that first brick on the eastern side.[21] Seven other bricks were laid by seven ministers of state and the ceremony over, he had gone to the north-east point of the circle where the Maha Thera Piyadassi stood.

'Stand beside me, O king,' Piyadassi had said, and then began to chant the *Jayamangala*.[22]

Why had not the relic chamber been completed. He had not taxed himself enough. He should have been more diligent. It had to be completed in order that the dome be finished. The cloud-coloured stones had been placed. These stones, of the largest size procurable, were without flaw. They had been brought in from India. One had been laid slab-wise on the flower-offering ledge in the centre, and four others made up the sides of the chamber while one had been kept aside to serve as the cover of the chamber. The brickwork soared up and around leaving an elevated platform connected to the terraces. 'Very soon,' he had told Tissa, and he had done so much. Why was it that as he grew weak and tired, the work also grew sluggish? He had been so overjoyed when the stones were brought. The samaneras Uttara and Sumana had been told to bring 'fat-coloured stones'.[23] They had gone to Uttarakuru in India for the stones, each one hundred feet square and eight finger-breadths thick. How carefully had these huge stones been borne. Elephants had dragged them on log rollers from the north.

The king was restless as he was borne back to the palace. In his chamber he grasped his brother's arm. 'Tomorrow,' he said. 'Tomorrow must the relic chamber be ready. We must place within it the relics before the waning of the moon. See to it, our brother.'

Tissa nodded. He saw the urgency in the dim eyes. 'My brother is very ill,' he thought. 'The waiting enfeebles him.' 'Tomorrow will it be,' he said and rushed away.

The *Mahavamsa* gives us a glorious picture of that day when the chamber was ready to receive the sacred objects. The four cloud-stones glowed on the sides and above, each in honour of the Gotama Buddha and the Buddhas Kassapa, Konagamana and Kakusanda. Duttha Gamani ascended the terraces, then descended into the relic chamber with slow, measured dignity. This was the first of his visits to the chamber and he wished it to be seen and noticed that his health was in no way impaired. No one could say with what effort the ailing monarch performed these duties of sheer love for the faith. He had achieved much and wished to be seen as the superhuman his subjects took him to be.

In the centre, he placed a replica of the Bodhi tree. Made of gold and gems, its silver trunk stood 18 cubits high, 8 inches in diameter and held five branches. Its roots were crafted in coral and it was fixed in a bed of sapphire. Every leaf was a gem, cunningly cut, and the faded leaves were of gold as were the fruits, while sprigs of coral twined lovingly. Around the roots was a sprinkling of emeralds. On the trunk were incised the eight auspicious symbols as well as an adornment of flowering creepers, animals and the sacred *hamsa*[24] and other birds. Over the tree, along the borders of the canopy hung little pearl bells and rows of golden chimes, all linked by chains, while at the four corners were hung pearls in strings and clusters. Upon the canopy were the motifs of the sun, moon and stars, set with gems of a citrine hue while the drapes were of diverse colours—a total of 1008 costly fabrics.

Surrounding the tree was a gem-studded railing, the enclosure paved with large pearls. Around this the king arranged rows of flower vases, each holding jewelled flowers of various hues. Bowls of water holding four perfumes, as well as silver containers holding the finest gems. On the terraces and platform the monks chanted, and around the stupa thousands gathered, each with a tray of precious offerings. Soft clouds coated the sun with fleece and a cooling breeze fanned the onlookers. East of the tree stood a throne which awaited the king's attention. It had been made of solid gold and was worth about ten million kahapanas. Upon it would be placed a carved composition of startling beauty, indeed the finest example of representational art, depicting the Buddha. Always, works of Buddhistic art had been non-representational—an empty throne, a lotus seat, the Bodhi tree, the footsteps graven on stone slabs, which designated the pilgrim path to worship, and the wheel of the Dhamma. Duttha Gamani had wished to bring artisans from abroad but the guild lord of the artisan community had asked the favour of creating the tableau.

'But such has never been done. Can you prepare such from the artist's impression?'

'Assuredly, lord king, and my craftsmen are willing.'

The artists made the first sketches and they were first engraved, then filled with charcoal and lime. Each large sketch needed to be scaled down. It had been part of Duttha Gamani's programme to call on the artisans, watch the careful fashioning of the precious tableau.

'When this work is done, no other such work will you do,' he had said. 'No work of any such sort, for this is to remain within the Maha Thupa. When you have done, none of the sketches must you retain.'[25] It was a resplendent piece of work. The Buddha in a sedent posture was of gold with body and limbs highlighted in gems of dive colours, artfully delineating the features and lines of the image. Among it stood figures of Maha Brahma, who bore the heavenly parasol of heavenly domination,[26] Sakkha, the king of the gods, holding a *chank*, as he anointed the Buddha, while Pancasikha, the minstrel of the gods played his lute.[27] The king of the Nagas, Kala Naga, was also represented with his band of singers and dancers and also the hundred-armed Mara with his elephants and servants.[28] Every figure was of pure gold and excellently rendered.

Having placed the tableau upon the golden throne, Duttha Gamani ordered the placing of seven other thrones which were as gleaming altars, each extremely costly—three on the three sides of the chamber, one in the north-easterly direction and three others to the south-west, south-east and north-west. It was a solemn yet glittering display of faith; a reliquary unequalled in beauty and riches. In each of the corners stood branches of coral surmounted with large gems and with clustering shoots of gold, pearl, lapis lazuli and green garnets. At the farthest points of the four sides stood carvings of the four great mythological kings: Dhatarattha, Virulha, Virupakkha and Vessavanna.[29]

Carl Muller

The carvings were stupendous in aspect and yet, as the *Mahavamsa* tells us:

> These offerings were arranged in the receptacle without crowding the space.

The chronicle attributes this to the supernatural agency of the king, the devas, and the arahat monks.

It may suffice to give here the description of these carvings as told in the *Mahavamsa*:

> [There were] thirty-three devas,[30] thirty-two princes and twenty chiefs of the Yakkhas. Above these devas, bowing down with clasped hands raised over their heads, still higher were others bearing vases filled with flowers, likewise dancing devatas, and devatas and devas playing instruments of music, and chanting devatas with mirrors in their hands, as well as those bearing bouquets of flowers and branches, devas with lotus blossoms and so forth, and other devas of many kinds and among them rows of arches made of gems and representations of the dhammachakra,[31] rows of sword-bearing devas and others bearing pitchers. Above their heads also were pitchers, five cubits high, filled with aromatic oil with wicks made of dakula fibres continually alight. In an arch of crystal there was in each of the four corners a great gem and moreover, in the four corners four glimmering heaps of gold, precious stones and pearls and of diamonds were placed. On the wall made of fat-coloured stones sparkling zigzag lines were traced,[32] serving as an adornment for the relic chamber.

All this had been arranged by the great thera Indagutta, to whom Duttha Gamani had given the task of supervision. The king had nothing but admiration for the manner in which it had all been contrived, and voiced his satisfaction. Why, there was even a couch representing the death of the Buddha, also adorned with various gems, so placed that its headrest faced the Bodhi tree.

'Venerable sir,' Duttha Gamani said to Indagutta, 'we are pleased beyond measure. And is there yet room for the paintings that will complete this hallowed receptacle?'

'There is space enough, O king, and the artists will be ready soon. It is necessary, I have said, that all should be done before long, for I have charged the ascetic Sonuttara to bring the relics of the Master. This will he do for he has the supernormal faculties to carry the drona hither.'

Duttha Gamani clasped his hands. 'Let the artists give of their best and as best they can—and yet, it is important that they complete their work in time.'

'Fear not, O king, for many scrolls are ready and await their outlining in gold and vermilion. It is the carbon black that takes some time.'[33]

'But will it all be ready?'

'Well within the appointed time.'

It would be well at this point to recount the manner in which the corporeal relics of the Buddha were apportioned—and it is well to return to India if only to remind ourselves that it was in that great land that the Sakyamuni strived so earnestly for the salvation of the world. It was on the shore of the Ganga one day that the Buddha and his followers saw Nanduttara, a Brahmin, who hurried up to make obeisance.

'Long have I awaited this opportunity, great sage,' he said. 'Give me leave to offer thee refreshment and to the brotherhood as well.'

The Buddha raised a hand in benediction and the Brahmin led them to his abode that was close to the landing place of Payaga. This spot, to many, held sacred significance, for there did the waters of the Ganga and Yamuna meet.

Having partaken frugally of what was offered, the Buddha turned to the thera Bhaddaji who had grown agitated by the remembrance of things past. 'You are concerned with thoughts of a past age, though it serves you little. But I see the flight of your mind. Is it that such memory is too sweet to put aside?'

The thera bowed. 'It is easy to put aside, master, but the waters bring it back and then it revolves in my mind as the waters do.'

'It is as it should be, O Bhaddaji, for it tells of the strength of those links that hold your many lives together. Let us speak of this again when we are upon the waters.'

'Do we then journey forth, master? Yet I see no ship.'

'Presently will a ship there be, and then will you see again the waters whirl as your mind does.'

Even the Brahmin Nanduttara exclaimed at the vessel that appeared, neared the landing place. He had much goods upon the water and knew of no ship that would be due for weeks. 'It is strange that a vessel comes at this unlikely time,' he remarked, 'for it stands high in the water and carries no cargo.'

The Buddha made a small gesture of acknowledgement. 'It is but a small craft and poorly fitted to meet the turmoil of two rivers. Yet, it will carry us for we have need to journey to the farther shore.'

The thera Bhaddaji peered over the wooden railings of the small vessel. Even as it stayed moored at the landing stage, it rocked alarmingly, skittish in the frothing rush of the river, being empty of hold. The other bhikkhus came to him, asked him why he looked so intently.

'See there,' he said, 'there—do you see where the water eddies and boils and spins? There below lies my palace. The palace I dwelt in when I was king in ages past.'

'A king? O brother of many virtues, do you recall your state in lives past?'

'I was one of many kings, O brothers, and the greatest of these was Mahasammata, from whose race was the master sprung. Know you not of the race of Mahasammata?'

'That we do, and many were the kings of that age,' said one.

'Aye brother,' said another. 'Have we not been told of those wondrous monarchs and princes of old at the time of the beginning of this kalpa? Do you say, brother, that in that time, you were one of those?'

'Aye, for I was of the dynasty of Mahasammata and my brother was Panada.'

'Then be you the incarnation of Mahapanada?'

'Aye, I was the king Maha Panada, and here, in the spot where the waters boil, below lies my palace. Twenty-five yojanas did it measure and it remains to remind me, for when the waters of the Ganga come upon it, it whirls and makes the waters troubled.'[34]

From all over the place, people flocked to the shore, crowded around the landing place, eager to see the Buddha. Many carried garlands while others bore offerings of cloth and aromatic oils. Some asked Nanduttara why he did not go with the great one, and what ship that was.

When on board the vessel, some of the brethren went to the master, their faces full of doubt. 'What is this that the thera Bhaddaji says. He would have us believe that he was a king even before thou were a king. We do not wish to believe this.'

'Banish your thoughts, O monks,' the master said, 'for the holy thera, schooled in all wisdom, tells but the truth of a life long past.'

But some of the brethren shook their heads. 'What then is this palace he says is his? Does it truly lie below? If it were as he says, readily will we believe him.'

The Buddha looked upon them tenderly. 'You understand not the powers of the blessed. Soon, with humility and acceptance will you too be endowed with such gifts as the saintly Bhaddaji possesses. Such powers, O monks, give us much to grieve over too, for there comes the memories of every day, of existences that reach back into a dim past where shadows only reside. Yet do we see all as clearly as if they are part of this present existence. I see that you are troubled as only sceptics are troubled. Do you then believe in me?'

'With all our hearts we do.'

'And do you also consult each other and say to one another that you can accept this and not that, that you can believe this and cannot believe that?'

The monks were silent. Then one said: 'But it is not you who makes such claim, master. It is the thera Bhaddaji who is not our leader.'

'And thus you reject his words...because he is not your master? Know this, O monks, the thera Bhaddaji walks in my footsteps and his saintliness is beyond doubt. Lo, I will banish your doubts...' and saying so, the Buddha rose, a dazzling figure in the air, swiftly ascending into the Brahma world, beyond the seven celestial realms, into the realms of form.[35] Then, carrying in one hand the Dussa Thupa, a reliquary of the Brahma world, he returned to hover over the ship so that all who gathered on the shore might see the wonder of the holy object. All around him rays of gold, green, orange and red streamed forth. On the pier, Nanduttara fell prostrate and cried: 'May I have such wondrous power that I could also go to the worlds beyond and bring back relics that may be venerated by all who live in this mortal realm.'

The Buddha laid a warm light on him. Dazedly the Brahmin heard a soft voice say, 'You will do so, good Nanduttara, not in this life but in another.'

The Buddha then returned the reliquary to the Brahma world and stood once again over the deck of the ship. Moving effortlessly over the whirlpool where the rivers rushed upon each other, he streaked into the depths and seized the palace of the ancient king Maha Panada, that lay there, its golden spire turning madly, churning the water. Rising with the monstrous edifice, he carried it high into the air so that all might look at it, then let it fall back into its grave. It was an awesome display of celestial might and yet, the Buddha stood again among his disciples, asking only that they not always seek for the things that they must see in order to bolster their faith. The vessel moved away and the people watched as the little group of yellow-robed men grew small in the distance. Only Nanduttara would not move. He lay there, dreaming of death and the life to come. It would be many, many lifetimes later that he would stand—the ascetic Sonuttara, in the Maha Vihara in Anuradhapura—a holy ascetic blessed with the same supernormal faculties as Bhaddaji of a long forgotten past.

It was the thera Indagutta, his spiritual head, who said to him: 'Your pious wish is granted.'

'But I have made no wish, great thera. It is not for the brethren to desire the least of things.'

Indagutta allowed himself a small smile. 'Ah, but you

have wished—wished that you would have the powers as of the master, have you not? So presumptuous were your thoughts then. Think back. Let your mind dissolve into the centuries past. Then will you know that what I say is true. I will leave you to your meditations but I will speak with you again before the sun descends.'

That evening it was Sonuttara who sought out Indagutta. 'Venerable one, I have given myself to desire when I was but a Brahmin trader of the landing place of Payaga. That was the holy place of Payaga as the people knew it to be, and I resided there. There did I see the master and saw with my eyes the wondrous power of his being.'

'That has been evident to me, for you entered the Order with special purpose. And who would blame you for the desire that rose within you?'

'Yet I know that it was improper. I sought to rise, move as the master would, take holy relics that lay in the hands of others.'

Indagutta closed his eyes, remained silent for a long time. Then he said, 'That is what you must now do. You are young. Sixteen years old are you, but none hold favour as you do in the sight of the devas. You must go, bring back the drona of relics that are destined to be enshrined here.'

'Gladly will I do so, venerable sir, but will I be able to procure such that others hold in their possession?'

'You must find a way, for it is the dying wish of the master. You must pit yourself against the mighty Nagas and thus will you know fulfilment of that desire you voiced so long ago.'

The young ascetic bowed. 'I will prepare myself and I will go forth…and I will return with that which is most precious.'

THE SERPENT WORLD

THE *MAHAVAMSA* TELLS US OF THE DYING WISHES OF THE BUDDHA with regard to the disposal of his corporeal relics. There has been some scholarly wrangling over the actual date of the Buddha's death, but the probable year is 483 BC, and this, it must be stressed, is approximate. In the Swat Valley was discovered a second century AD relief of the death scene, sublimely crafted, Sakkha, the king of the gods, stands beside the eighty-year-old sage, while in all the celestial worlds beings both formless and with form pour forth their hymns of praise upon the one who had broken the bounds of mortality and ascended that shining triple ladder to stand above the heavenly throne.

It was to Sakkha that the Buddha made his dying request. 'O king of the gods,' he whispered, 'of the eight dronas of my bodily relics, let one drona be adored first by the Koliyas[36] of Ramagama.'

Sakkha bent low to show the master that he was attentive to the words. The Buddha remained still for a moment, and continued. 'Then will this drona be borne to the kingdom of the Nagas where all will adore it, but at the last it must be borne to Lanka where it shall be enshrined in a Great Thupa that a king will cause to be built.'

Of the other seven dronas, the Buddha told the thera Mahakassapa that these would be divided by the king Dhammasoka.[37] It was left to Mahakassapa to safeguard the relics. He was the chief thera after the Buddha's death and head of the First Buddhist Council and, under his leadership, the truths and teachings of the Buddha were compiled and the furtherance of the doctrine assured.

Mahakassapa saw to it that a great amount of the relics, full seven dronas, be held near Rajagaha, the capital of king Ajatasattu; but when he brought these to Asoka, he made sure that the drona in Ramagama remained there as the Buddha had wished. Asoka had been amazed at the wealth of relics brought to him. He all but choked with emotion and was overjoyed to know that he could distribute these to all the temples and places of worship he had built. 'If there were more, how much more could we do,' he had cried, 'for with each relic we bestow will we spread the light of the doctrine.'

The ascetics remained silent for they knew that the emperor would soon discern that all the relics had not been delivered. It was just as they feared. Asoka examined the relics and a line furrowed his brow. 'But there has to be more! Here are seven dronas. What of the eighth? Why has it not been brought here?'

'That is retained at the stupa of Ramagama, lord,' an ascetic said. 'This have we done according to the instructions of the Maha Thera Mahakassapa, and that too, according to the wishes of the enlightened one.'

'And where, say you, that these wishes have been recorded? And will one drona serve a single stupa while it is our need to apportion what is here to over a thousand? We feel that this is not the manner of true and just apportioning. Let the relics of Rajagama be brought hither.'

But the monks prevailed. 'What truer apportioning is there, lord, when thou hast seven dronas to divide and one remains to be worshipped at Ramagama, and then in the world of the Nagas and finally in the great thupa that will be built in the island beyond the waters? It is not to thee that the eighth drona is given. Would you not accept that the king of gods was witness to this bequeathal? Do not earn the displeasure of the devas, lord, for thy acceptance of the will of the master brings thee much merit.'

Asoka inclined his head. 'We understand,' he said, and no more did he ask after the relics he could not have.

The rains came in due time but with a fury that had never been known of before. The rivers rose and swamped the forests of the Gangetic plain. In the terai[38] the drongos called out in panic and wild buffaloes climbed to the safety of the dolomite rises. Everywhere the burrows of porcupines and otters, the nesting holes of sand martins and kingfishers were inundated, and everywhere the *kha-ko* of langurs resounded as they sped away to safety.

In Ramagama, the stupa that held the eighth drona of relics could not withstand the onslaught of the waters. Slowly, the brickwork began to collapse and even as the people began to run for their lives, the relic chamber was exposed and the waters licked in to take the urn, sweep it away. The rushing course carried it down, the strong current tossed it in a boiling torment of mud-brown and grey-green until, far down the plains, the bloated river rolled its girth to meet the ocean.

The havoc of the coastal plains was terrible. Blind rivers[39] streamed in, added their weight to the marshy deltas between the Damodar and the Hooghly. The savannah lay

Carl Muller

beneath the flood while wild boar, chital and elephants sped to higher ground. It is characteristic of the region that the sea also makes its way inland through a number of creeks, sweeping the tidal swamps and forests. The urn, miraculously undamaged, moved upon the crests. Then, where river and ocean roared at each other and the clouds seemed to press their bellies upon the mud flats, the urn rose, standing upright in the sullen air. Suddenly the rain ceased, and far out to sea, the sun spread a coat of molten blue-white, soothing the tempest of wave and white cap. On land too there was a lull as the waters moved in a softer, oily motion. As the clouds fled, a great ball of light danced down, then shivered into fingers of saffron, lavender, emerald, crimsom and sparkling white fire. The rays pulsed, picking swathes of colour on the surface of the sea, then swirled around the urn. The gold of its surface burst into a brilliant riot of colour and, as at a signal, the sea swept back and the rivers turned tail and there, in the great cleft that appeared, and which was both seabed and river bed, lay the gateway to the Naga world where stood a throne of reddened gold. Its head was encrusted with a massed field of gems and so was each arm. The legs were marvellously fashioned, each of them held within the coiling embrace of a golden serpent. Around the arms too were diamond-studded heads of rearing cobras. The seat and back were of plush velvet that glowed like the rarest wine. Slowly, the urn descended, the colours of its aureole spearing the walls of water, of sea and river that had parted. It rested gently on the throne.

At the bottom of this immense funnel was a dark portal—a forbidding cave mouth within which Naga guardsmen stood. They had backed away, standing in fear deep within the cave, staring in awe at the blazing glory of the throne. Even as the urn descended, its many-coloured lights shivered within the cave, and they had stumbled back. They had entered the cave from its broad rear entrance when the water in the upper chamber had begun to suck out. They had come warily, for the water had always remained to protect their world from those who sought it. As serpents, they could cleave the water whenever they wished to fare into the world above, but none could find the way into their domain. It was a shock to see the water drain away and had rushed up the path into the rocky basin. The walls of the cavern were slimy, but with serpentine ease they worked their way to the outer mouth and stood gasping.

''Tis a gift,' one said. 'A gift from the gods.'

'Assuredly,' the other hissed. 'And see above…the waters have parted. Some force holds them back.'

'Away, away!' another cried. 'The king must be told of this. We must hurry. What if the waters come together? All will be lost and we will surely drown.'

Down the long basin they sped, took the inner road deep under the ocean until it widened, and suddenly there was open country—a world below a world—with shining streets and rich dwellings and lordly avenues where columns of alabaster and coral held beautifully carved serpents with shining stones in their heads. In open courtyards of crystalline rock, Naga maidens danced and sang and twined their arms and swayed as their jewelled girdles glinted in the light of a thousand torches.

A sunless, subterranean world…yet had the Nagas brought all they had need of: horses, elephants, chariots, musical instruments. Far in the reaches of the kingdom were laid fields of delicate grass and all around were the giant crystal mirrors that gave light as from the sun so that trees might take hold and vines might grow and fruits and flowers flourish. Cattle too did they have, and from the floor did they bring forth water—cold, pure and laced with life-giving minerals. Long channels carried the water to all the cities of their world and the most resplendent was Manjerika, where the king of the Nagas had his palace.

Kala Naga, the king was astonished. 'A throne? And an urn of gold that gives forth rays of light?' He summoned his chieftains and the wise men. He had no fears that his domain would be discovered. The way into the Naga world lay open, but who would dare enter? His wise old advisers nodded solemnly. They were very old. Their faces had shrunken, were heavily lined and they had long forsaken their human form, being too old to move on their legs. Yet, in all the worlds, none as wise as they.

'The throne and the urn they say of is ours, O king,' they said. 'These are sent us just as the great teacher of the Sakya desired. Now in death does he remain, poised over the many world systems, the greatest of all the celestials. In the urn are relics of his human form. We must convey these hither, make of them the objects of unceasing devotion.'

'It is a gesture of acknowledgement, O king,' said another, 'for are we not sprung from the great serpent of infinity whom we adore as the sacred Ananta? Always have the gods of the worlds on high considered the Naga as the symbol of divinity, of rebirth, of mystery and of infinity.'

'But, wise ones, do we not also bow to the Purusha who is named Vishnu and is lord of the celestials and master of the Nagas?'

'That we also do, O king, but who can yet say why you yourself was impelled to leave this domain that you might remain in serpent form beside the tree at Gaya where the Buddha awaited the crossing into light? And there, O Kala Naga, did you not give your blessing to the serene one?'

'That did we do, for even here did not the seabed tremble because of the power of his will?'[40]

'Yes, and we of the moisture-born[41] who are the true Nagas of this world below...and the worlds above have ever befriended the Sakyamuni; did not the great Mucalinda shelter the master? Have we not always served the gods and the teachers of the gods? Did not Vishnu Narayana use the canopy of the earth-bearing Naga to sleep in? Are we not of the garland of Siva and the weapon of Ganesa? But never has one of the womb-born been permitted to become a part of the Order of the Bretheren.'

'That do we know, but scarcely can we fault it, for truly are the womb-born of ruder culture and less development both in habit and accomplishment.'[42]

'That is true, O king, and yet do we see that the master held great esteem and favoured us much. This throne, the urn, are given to us to be honoured.'

King Kala Naga rose. 'Let all assemble. Hasten! Sound the horns and beat the drums. Let a central site be prepared and see that the builders construct a platform with five steps leading to it from each of the four sides. Then let the masons prepare a circle for inner worship, yet another for offerings, yet another for outer worship and yet another to serve as the approaches. Let it all be done without delay. Flag-bearers must we have and the standards of silver with the coiling serpent...ah, maidens! Yes, maidens with silver pitchers and maidens in serpent form as well. Lead forth the horses and the elephants to accompany the relics when we are at the gates. A thousand will we need to go to the approaches...and carrying poles, yes, carrying poles and fine linen ropes. See that nothing is overlooked.'

Duttha Gamani consulted the astrologers. 'The monks have assured us that the sacred relics will be brought hither. Give ye the date of the enshrinement, for all must be made ready.'

It was indeed to be readied…the whole city and the road leading to the Maha Vihara to be decorated; all tradesmen and the town dwellers to be dressed in festive attire. At the four gates would imposing *thoranas*[43] be erected. Also at the gates would be placed ample quantities of cloth and food for all who would enter.

Over several days, monks of India had arrived in the most mysterious ways and none could say how they came. Many in the city marvelled and whispered of strange sights in the sky around the Bo tree as well as the Brazen Palace. They told of lights that wheeled around but others claimed they saw saffron-robed beings who seemed to descend in bubbles of light.

'So many monks,' Duttha Gamani exclaimed. 'The brethren come in from everywhere. We have watched them pour in at the gates—from Ruhuna and the Malaya region, from Nagadipa and Kalyani, even from Paccinadipa[44]—and yet, how many come from across the water…' He broke off as a cough racked him.

Tissa was concerned. 'Do not excite yourself. You need to rest now. Yes, more than ever, for much will you have to do on the day of the enshrinement.'

'A slight cough, brother. That is all. What a burdensome thing this is, to be a king, when a little cough causes such concern.' He drank the water offered him, coughed again and cleared his throat. 'Yes, but tell us, is it true that monks have been seen hovering in the air and arriving in aerial cars the colour of the moon?'

'All over the land do people tell of such. I have also seen splendid lights around the Bodhi tree. What is more, no ships have carried these visitor monks here and yet, so many there are. Brother, this is yet another manifestation of the wonders of the faith. As you have directed, there is place for them all within the apartments of the Lovamahapaya, and that is where they remain.'

'See that alms are given unceasingly and that robes be presented to all who come.[45] Also brother, the order of the procession must be checked. The astrologers say that in number, there must be one thousand and eight women of beauty who must bear the pitchers of perfumed oils and water around the *mangalaratha*.[46] Have we such a number?'

'Assuredly. Rest you even for a while. I will see that all is done.'

'Your presence is a comfort, brother, and so reassuring. Yes, we will rest awhile.'

Tissa summoned the ministers to the council chamber. 'The coming of the relics require all honours as due to royalty,' he said, and it is necessary that the monarch be attended by all his troops. In full armour must they be and each will bear a flowing silk on his lance. The elephants must be dressed in cloth of gold, and see to it that the stables provide the finest pure-white Sindhu horses[47] to draw the car of the state. We are told that the king wishes a special role for his beloved elephant Kandula. The beast must be sumptuously adorned, and let his rider carry a white parasol. Mark you, the astrologers have deemed the number 1008 to be propitious for both the day and the occasion. It is the wish of the king that this number of maidens must accompany the state car with silver pitchers of aromatic substances. Let there be a like number to be flower-bearers and a like number with lanterns. Also a like number of young boys bearing flags. All this must be made ready at once and see that the goldsmiths fashion a handsome casket that the king's elephant may carry as a symbol of the honour it pays to the relics. Is this all understood?'

The ministers agreed that the arrangements were suited to the occasion. 'Beaters will range the kingdom assembling all who are needed, lord. It is fitting that the maidens be gathered from all the land.'

'It is. Dispatch riders to Ruhuna, Dighavapi, Uruvela, Kalyani, even to Bhallatittha[48] if need be. It is well that there is representation of all regions for even now are we informed that the whole land has been adorned in honour of the coming of the sacred relics. Yes, let all share the joy.'

'Even now do people pour in from all parts, lord. The chieftains have begun the construction of encampments along the banks of the Kadambanadi and the Gonanadi.'[49]

'That is good. Also can dwelling places be readied along the road to the Missaka Mountain[50] and at Cetavigama[51] and around Dovarikamandala. Wherever such are built, ensure that there is sufficient water.'

'And what part does the prince Saliya play, O king. We have made arrangements that a special procession lead the prince from the western palace.'

'That is well. We will consult our brother. He may wish that the prince ride with him. But he must be conveyed with all honour befitting the viceroy of the land from the western sector he now rules. See that this is done.'

The young ascetic Sonuttara sat in his cell, his face pale and drawn. Never had be been faced with such a task as this. He had to enter the Naga world, also enter into that state where he would begin to feel the lack of material body, of total unreality and depersonalization. The practice was dangerous, that he knew, for there could come accompanying delusions and hallucinations and the risk of losing all touch with reality.[52]

Sonuttara needed to be as a serpent, in order to penetrate the world of the serpent people. He needed to charge himself with a flexibility to reach out to immense distances, to be as supple as the snake and see into the minds of the snake people who had the facility to glide their thoughts, one into the other, just as serpents would weave together in a single writhing mass.

Sonuttara knew how the Nagas in their snake form filled people with awe, respect, even fear. No, it was no myth, for those of the Naga world were semi-divine and could change forms at will.[53] He had considered the yoga of automatism where his functions would slip the controlling reins of his conscious self. In this way, his limbs, head, tongue, could move beyond conscious will; but he rejected this as being unsuitable to his task. There would be too much physical disassociation and a remoteness that would not permit him to plan his moves.[54]

He began the exercises of Prana yoga[55] knowing that this was the first step towards psychic power.[56] Long had he used the arts of meditation, concentration and contemplation, for was this not the way the master had attained serenity, awareness and wisdom? The arahats had schooled him well. Even at fourteen, Sonuttara could use his powers to project his mind. Yes, he knew now what he must do. He lay upon the rug in his cell and allowed the forces within him to rise. He could now hear the sounds of the world below, the bells of animal harnesses, the tramp of elephants,

Carl Muller

the sound of sing-song voices, the tread of thousands as they circled the relics of the master.[57]

Yes, it was time to go. What was necessary was travelling clairvoyance, or going forth astrally. His breathing became shallow, then but a wispy murmur. Now could his astral body rely on thought forms wherever his mind would project his wishes, making them of a visible form on the astral plane. Thus could he simply wish for what he wanted and be able to reach out and seize it.[58]

The cell dazzled as the other self emerged, rose, and in a whirl of smoking silver plunged into the floor. Nothing could bar its way, not gravel or shale, stone or rock. All over its snaking form exploded starbursts of silver as it drove deep, deeper and finally whirled to make a level path, moving at incredible speed. It then began to stream upwards. Even as it hurtled on, it became charged with a sensibility that flowed along the silver ribbon that joined it to the young ascetic who lay in his cell as one dead. This force, to the astral, was an all-inclusive psychic sense.[59]

In the cell, it seemed that Sonuttara's breathing had ceased altogether. The arahat Indagutta entered barefooted. He bent over the form of the boy, saw the thread of silver snake out of his forehead, disappear into the cold stone of the floor. Another monk, torch in hand, stood at the door. 'He is in the state of samadhi,'[60] Indagutta said. 'I hope he has not rushed through the preceding stages. He will bring back what his mind desires.'[61]

'His face is drawn and there is some anguish in it,' the monk at the door whispered.

'Aye, but these are but the signs of emotion at the going away of self. He feels more since he is so young, but I have no doubt that he will succeed. I will sit by him. Do not bring the torch into the room. You may stay with us if you will.'

Slowly, the minutes crept by. Around the Bo tree the devas awaited and the night was hushed. Even the owls and bats were silent and in the temples, even on the rise of Mihintale, monks sat, cross-legged, silently awaiting the hour.

In the world of the Nagas, a silver being seemed to flash upon the floor of the king's hall of assembly, and then stood, a young clear-eyed monk. Kala Naga rose, astonished. How had this being penetrated the earth, the ocean? Or had he plunged down the chasm of the parted waters? But no, for even as the throne and the urn had been drawn in, borne to the city, the great basin had filled. The waters above had met and none could find their way to the doors.

Kala Naga waved to a seat beside his throne. The monk walked up, stood before the Naga lord.

'The relics that are here, brought out of the parted waters, and that are now in thy hands, and that your people even now make obeisance to…these relics are appointed by the Buddha to be enshrined in the Great Thupa of Lanka. From there have I come to carry back what must be enshrined there. Do thou give them to me, O king, for the allotted time given thee to worship them—three full moons—have been fulfilled. I have been sent to take the urn away from here.'

All around were the indignant hisses of the assembled serpent beings. Sonuttara sensed the displeasure they felt and the anger that sat in the king's mind. He made his form grow until he stood as a towering figure, glowing with silver light.

'Do thou give them to me,' he said again, and his voice rang in the great vaulted chamber.

THE PRINCESS-ELECT

SALIYA BROUGHT HIS HORSE TO A WALK AS THEY REACHED THE broader approach to the eastern quarter. He wore a look of stern pride, but yet Devi could feel the tenseness of his arm around her. His forearm moved to lie across her breast and she felt the pressure of his arm tightening. She wanted to turn her head to him, ask him why he had lessened the pace of the horse, but she remained still. So imprisoned, she stared at the side of the road.

'No more will you move around the city as you are,' he said.

'My prince, what is this you say?'

'As my princess will you be, and garbed as a princess. No more must you remain uncovered as you now are. It is only for me to uncover you.'

Devi paled. She knew that the prince was challenging social norms, and he seemed to be determined to carry the challenge all the way. She opened her lips to speak but could not. Instead, she gave a little sigh. This was his battle. He would defy his father, law, custom. He needed to be loved as never before for he would have to fight alone. She would remain a chandala—and what would he be?

They were first seen by one man, then a group of

men, then as they neared the walls, by hundreds. The cries of amazement, even of anger arose, and men sped to the citadel and women rushed around calling to their neighbours. Saliya drew on the reins. Men who followed furtively, stopped, tried to edge away. From behind the fences of compounds, people nudged each other, hissed their anger, gesticulated. The air hissed with the sound of scolding female voices.

'What is this unseemly show?' Saliya shouted. 'Have you not seen your prince upon a horse before?'

There was no answer. Saliya moved. A hush descended around him but ahead was the drone of voices and indignant cries and shouts. Outside the citadel there rose a pandemonium of outraged citizens who rushed to convey the news to the palace. Guards were pressed for entry by the shouting men and women who shrilled imprecations on the outcast.

In the Helloli village, Devi's father looked at his wife with panic. 'We are undone,' he grated. 'Our Devi! Weep, woman, weep! Pluck out your eyes! She has brought pollution upon the prince. Now will we surely die.'

Devi's mother lay, her body heaving. She had broken the water pots and stamped upon the sharp shards. With hair streaming, she had beaten her face into the sand. She moaned horribly, her face scraped and raw, her soles bleeding.

'Rise woman, we must flee. We must go to the river, hide among the rushes…no, we must go to Mundavaka.'

A large stone crashed against the mud walls of the house. Devi's mother jerked to her knees, twisting at the cloth that was unknotted at her waist. Her breasts were daubed with sand and there was spittle on her chin. Another stone fell, then another. She gave a broken scream. Her husband hauled her up. 'Go! Go to the fence through the thorn grass. They stone us, the people. See, the others also flee…Go!'

All over the chandala quarter were scenes of panic. Confused, frightened, the outcastes glared murderously at Devi's parents who also ran with them. 'Were you not aware of the ripening of your daughter,' one snarled, 'and you our chief. Is this how you have protected us? The people stone our homes. Who is to say what evil they intend.'

'They will burn our homes,' a woman sobbed. 'I heard some men say so outside the fence.'

Devi's father stopped, stood against a cluster of rocks. Above, the sky was deepening and crows wheeled in spatters of black beyond the line of fences. 'My woman and I go,' he said, 'and we will take the riverbank to the region of the great river and then to Mundavaka where chandalas of the crafts live untroubled. Why must you flee? What wrong have you done that you run away? Lay your curses on us if you must, but what wrong have you done? Tell me that.'

'It is your daughter. The slut! Why did you not give her to one of us? Did your woman accompany her when she went each day to the groves? Did your woman not know her slut's mind?'

Devi's mother screamed, launched herself at the speaker, clawing wildly. 'You! You! You dare to call my daughter a slut—you who ravish your aged mother!' They rolled in the thorn grass and others leaped to drag them apart.

Devi's father leaped to a tree, found a stout, dry fallen branch. He swung fiercely and the man fell, blood streaming from a gash over his ear. Brandishing his cudgel, he stood over his woman. 'I am your chief,' he shouted, 'and I tell you to go back. And yes, we will return with you. But we will go the way my daughter always went—there, to the wall that stands beside the Asoka trees. We will call to the prince, tell of the injustice done to us. Have we not a right to be heard? Where does the prince take my daughter—to his palace in the southern street? There, where the Asoka trees are? There will we go. The prince is a good man, is he not? What kindness has he shown us who are the lowest of the low. And he takes my daughter to his palace. He shows her honour, does he not? Easily could he have treated her as some of you women have been used by the traders! What? Do you say nay? How many men of standing have you given yourselves to...yes, you!' he pointed to a dark-skinned woman of thirty. 'Do we not know how our women offer their bodies for the goods they have not the coin to buy? And did we point and call them sluts? Come, I will lead you, tell the prince of our plight. Let him bring order. Surely the prince will see that we only wish to live in this city as we have always done. And who will scavenge and keep the streets clean and the toilets emptied? Think you the people have no need of us that they wish to burn our homes?'

There was a muttering among the men, but they saw the wisdom of their chief's words. 'But you say you go to Mundavaka,' one said.

'I did—and I see it as better that we do. But I will ensure that all is well before we leave. Don't you see how impossible it will be for me and my woman? And I will tell the prince that if he does not take my daughter to be his consort, he must send her back to me. Come, is this not what any man would do if he were in my place? I will be as a chief. If my daughter returns, sent back to me, I will still honour my prince. Never must it be said that he wished a chandala for his wife. Never will he be reminded of it. I will kill her, my woman and myself! Is that enough for you? Let us now go where the Asoka trees are. To the southern wall!

They went.

❖

Duttha Gamani was shocked. 'What? Does he parade this woman on his horse through the city?'

The chief minister saw anger, no, a look of horror in the king's eyes. It was necessary to calm him, for it was known that the king was ailing and was not to be upset. But what could he do? A situation such as this could not be hidden. As it was, hundreds of citizens stood at the gates. Soon, the guild lords and the chieftains would come to make protest. The prince had taken the woman to the southern palace. The guards there stood fast, even threatened the people who sought the gates. No, it was only the king who could intervene.

Tissa, on being told, had taken a strong horse guard, ordered the people to return to their homes. He was angry. Soon, he knew, the holy relics would be brought. It was to be a day of national rejoicing. Now, the people regarded the chandala quarter, the Helloli village with baleful eyes. He rode into the mob, ordered the people off the streets.

'What is it you intend!' he roared. 'Burn this quarter? Fools! Do you not see the outcastes have fled? And do you condemn them all? Back! Back to your homes, and let no one show his face in the street. The king will resolve this! It is not for you to act! Any harm you do is in defiance of the authority of the king and will merit punishment!'

The people oozed away and Tissa told a commander.

'Take men. Find out where the chandala hide. See that they return. Assure them that they will come to no harm.'

Duttha Gamani sat, looking bleakly at his hands and his mind filled with thoughts of long ago. *He* was the disobedient one. How had he insulted his father, called him coward, even sent him a woman's garments to wear. And Kavan Tissa had suffered the scorn and whiplash of his son's words.[62] And now this shame his son had heaped on him. He blamed himself. He should have ensured a fitting consort, a princess for Saliya. He had been too engrossed in the work on the Maha Thupa. Yes, he had made Saliya viceroy. He wished the boy to succeed him…all the more reason he should have given the boy a bride. 'A chandala,' he muttered. 'Has he lost his mind?' He clapped his hands. 'Summon the lady Madri who is the wife of the chieftain of Viharabijagama.[63] She it was who taught the prince many arts and skills and he holds her in much esteem. We wish her to ascertain how matters really stand.'

Madri Devi was a woman much acclaimed among the ladies of the palace. Vihara Maha Devi would turn to her when there was need to decorate the royal chambers. Her skills were known in all the kingdom, and Prince Saliya admired her tremendously. She came before the king, accompanied by her husband Udena.

Duttha Gamani accepted their greetings and said. 'It is to the lady Madri that this task is given. Do you, Udena, accompany her to the southern palace of the prince, and she must go in alone and seek audience with him. She must learn of how matters stand. She must gain all knowledge of this chandala he has taken therein. You, lady Madri, must also say to the prince that it is our wish that he take the crown at the given time. This is our wish, and as future king, he must be wed to one of royal line

46   Carl Muller

or from a Brahmin family and of the noblest caste.' He brought his hand down sharply. 'He must renounce this casteless woman! He defiles the royal line. In our love for him and with patience we ask that he sees reason. Say this to him and convey to us what he says in reply.'

'I will do all I can, great one.'

'Do so. Go now. Also, it may be told that if it be but his desire that he wishes to satisfy, he may do so and we will give this woman much coin to take away with her. Also will we settle her and her parents on the other side of the river that they set no foot in the city. But renounce her he must! He brings pain and shame upon us.'

Saliya, with Asokamala Devi beside him, listened to the lady Madri and laughed. 'Does my father think that I take this maid but to appease the fire of my loins? That have I done, and that will I do each day at the time of waking and of sleeping. You, my lady, who know me so well… have we not talked of art as the desire of the soul? And what of love and the desires of the one who loves? What is this you say? Renounce her? Never! Rather would I be an outcaste as she is. Rather will I renounce all this and live among the chandala. Will you say this to the king?'

Lady Madri was distressed. 'But you are to be king. Yours will be the seat of the lion.'

'Aye, that can I accept—but even on the Lion Throne will she sit beside me,' and he took Devi's hand, caressed it. 'Look on her. She is virtuous. She is the most beautiful in all the land. If a pregnant woman who is desirous of ripe pomegranates is given the finest honey-sweet mangoes, will they satisfy her? Likewise must I satisfy the desire of my heart. Go ye, tell my father that even if he were to bring to me a divine maiden, she would not fulfil my heart's desire. Look. Look upon her. Can you, who taught me of all things beautiful, my teacher of the most delicate of arts, can you not see how wondrous a being she is? How can even a forest of lotus flowers which delight in the rays of the sun, give of their promise to the cold rays of the moon?

'And say also to my father that he demands of me even what the Buddha would not ask. Is not this system of high- and low-born deplorable in the eyes of the true followers of the Buddha? Does my father deny the strictures of the Lord Buddha he so honours? Yes, convey this to him for I wish him to know that he does me ill in asking of me such an impossibility. Gladly will I leave this kingdom. Gladly will I renounce the throne that is offered me. Gladly will I seek my destiny with this maiden of my choice. My father is wrong, and he must be made aware of the wrong he does.'

Madri Devi looked at the couple helplessly. She saw the chandala maid, her eyes downcast, a figure of exceeding loveliness. She sensed the girl's fear, but even in these crucial moments nothing could dim the radiance of her beauty. Madri marvelled. Could she truly be a chandala? What an astoundingly lovely princess she would be. But she already was…the choice of the prince. Bowing, she left and her husband took her back to the king.

She made sure to convey all that the prince had said and Duttha Gamani was troubled. His son had challenged him, even challenged his faith. He needed to be assured. 'We must consult with the theras,' he said.

In all the world, the Sinhalese are the only Buddhists to nurture a system of caste. True, there is some semblance of caste in Burma, but as Hutton[64] points out, this does not constitute a caste system. What is important to remember, and pertaining to the issue raised by prince Saliya, is that the Buddha had made it quite clear that:

No man is by birth an outcaste and by deeds is one a Brahmin.

Many texts of antiquity tell of the Buddha's ruling that the ultimate enlightenment is no prerogative of caste or social status. What is necessary is that one lives in accord with the truths and precepts of Buddhism. Fick[65] insists that even the priesthood is intended as no monopoly of the high caste, and even untouchables are admissable. In the *Sutta Nipata* translated by Hare[66] we have the following:

And the Master spake thus:

The evil angry man
Man if ill-will and cant
Deceitful, base in view
Know him as outcaste vile...

No outcaste is by birth,
No Brahmin is by birth:
By deeds an outcaste he,
By deeds a Brahmin he!

In fact, as Ryan[67] tells us, Brahminic pretensions and hypocrisy were favourite targets for the Buddha in his denunciation of sinful or unmeritorious behaviour. However, as Law[68] points out, Buddhism had little effect upon the Indian caste structure and indeed held no conflict with it. In fact, Buddhists accepted blood purity and familial prestige, and to this day, the Sangha remains an organization that embodies and practises caste principles. In fact, there was a formal edict during the reign of King Kirthi Sri Rajasinghe, a Malabari king of Kandy in later centuries[69] which established the Siyam Nikaya (the Siamese sect of priests) as a monopoly of the higher caste of cultivators.[70]

The monks were most insistent. Blood and honour must be protected. 'It is not for the prince to interpret the Buddhistic law, O king,' said the Maha Thera. 'It needs be that when the prince has tired of this dalliance, the female must be seized and made as a slave to the people.'

Duttha Gamani could not believe what he was hearing. 'But tell us, good sirs, did or did not the Buddha preach against the system we now uphold?'

'We could dwell long on this matter, O king, but it is surely so that the Master accepted the social system. There is a discourse of the Master that reveals what was truly intended. You are perturbed, sire, at the manner of the prince's words, but the prince has not given himself to a greater understanding of the Master's words. The Master has said that one must offer salutations to those who ought to be saluted and one must give up his seat to another more worthy. If one shows neither honour, respect, deference nor worship to those who are so entitled, will the offender suffer misery at death and woe in purgatory, and being reborn will he be one of a low and unimportant family. Thus does the doctrine tell of the law of *kamma*[71] and in truth, great one, one's birth status and position stand at the very core of the Master's teaching.'

'But does not the prince say that caste is not of the Buddha? How is that, and is that true?'

'Only as far as the Master has pronounced. What is meant is that caste is of no value for the attainment of *nibbana*.[72] Even the Master voiced his preference for being born a Kshatriya[73] in his denouncement of the ills of the Brahmins.'

'We are confused, good sirs, for is it that you now say

Carl Muller

that the doctrine is that of a revolution? Do we not give great honour to the Brahmins?'

'O king, there is no revolution, as you say. But what doctrine can survive without a social thought? And such thought has no conflict with caste. It is the prince who seeks to confuse and thus justify himself. The Master showed his abhorrence for the corruption of the Brahmins, not for their status.'

'We will think upon this. Yet, as you say, the maiden is a chandala because of her kamma. Is it not likely then that she was of the high-born in her previous life?'

'That is possible, yes, but it does not take away the fact that she is of the lowest now. Who can dismiss the effects of kamma? And who dares rebel against the state of present being. For is this not the will of the gods?'

When the monks had gone, Duttha Gamani told Tissa. 'It would seem that the brotherhood condemns our son too. In the city the people condemn him. Throughout the land will the news course and there will be many who will look upon us as being weak and giving face to such perfidy. We are grieved, brother, and this burden is heavy for we see it as a visitation of our own kamma. Scorn of our father brings upon us the scorn of our son.'

'Do not distress yourself, brother. You are lord of this land. If you would accept this maiden as high-born, merely crossed by the effect of kamma, would not that appease the people?'

The king sat up, startled. 'What? Can we really do so?'

Tissa shrugged. 'Such has never been done before. No, it is a precedent of much danger. There will follow a disruption of all of the social order.'

'Yes, yes, but brother, your words have aroused me...'
He clapped his hands, told the chamberlain. 'Send for the wise ones. It is urgent, tell them so.'

Tissa frowned. 'What does my brother intend?'

'Hush. You must accompany them…ah, they come. Virtuous Brahmins, with our brother the king must you go to the southern palace of the prince. You must examine the signs upon the body of the chandala maiden. Let not her beauty be all you take note of, but discover what fortunate signs there be.'

'And if the signs are poor?' Tissa asked.

'Then will she be banished. Then will we order her seized and she will leave this kingdom naked and at spear point! And our son may go with her in like state if that is what he desires!'

Saliya went to the chandala who stood at the walls. 'You are assured that the maid remains as my consort. You, who know not what honour is can now know honour, for one among you have I chosen. The king does not wish it and so do I forego claim to the kingship; for never will I be king without the maid Devi as my queen. Go back to your homes, and you, the parents of my princess, accept all that I send out to you. There is coin enough to last you all your days and a wagon with all you will need to sustain you. Find a new home, for that is my wish.'

'Lord, it is our intention to retire to Mundavaka, beyond the great river.'

'Do so, and make sure that your home is large and there is a place where I may rest my head.'

'But, gracious one…'

'Enough. Disperse now. See, the wagon comes. Know you that even as I choose among you, so can I live among you if needs be. Go now, and fear no more.'

Carl Muller

'Will our daughter take leave of us, lord?'

'If she must, I will bring her to you.'

Saliya watched the quiet parting. There were no tears. Many stood closely around with solemn faces. Others looked upon the contents of the wagon and nodded when they were told that the goods would be shared among them. When they moved away Devi felt the tears trickle down her cheeks. 'I will not see them again,' she said.

Saliya drew her to him, held her close. 'See how the Asoka flowers have fallen. It is as if each tree stands in its own blood. Ah, but there has been no one to pick them today.'

They lay in each other's arms that night, making love in a long, tender fashion. It was only when the pond herons swept out of their resting places to skim the waters of the Tissa Wewa that they fell asleep, locked within each other. The sound of the drawing of the gates woke him. Outside the chamber, valets, attendants, servants of the household waited. A courtier said, 'Tell the prince that a group of the king's wise ones have arrived on the orders of the palace.'

The master of the household nodded.

Saliya rose swiftly. Devi, naked, curled up, her knees drawn up, her buttocks thrust towards him, her black hair spread across her pillow, inflamed him. He positioned himself against her and gently eased his penis into her. She stirred, then put a hand back to clasp his hip. He felt her press against him as he drove hurriedly into her. 'This is for me,' he said, breathing hard as he spent himself. 'Now must I prepare to meet whatever else my father sends, for surely has he done so.'

Rising, he placed a coverlet over her. 'I will send a serving maid to tend you.'

With his attendants, he descended to the bath. When

told of the Brahmins and the arrival of his uncle, he nodded. 'Offer them refreshment. I will see them in the assembly hall.'

Devi watched the serving woman lay a jewelled girdle upon the bed. 'Am I to wear this too?'

'Yes. It is what our lord wishes.' The voice was clipped, disapproving.

Much used to scorn, used to the ostracism that had been part of her existence, Devi did not really see the flash of distaste in the woman's eyes.

'Is it that I must tend you while you garb yourself?' the woman asked.

'It is not necessary. I must bathe and await the prince.'

'He will be busy. The Brahmins await him, and the king Tissa. Soon will they convince the prince.'

Convince? Devi thought: convince of what? Suddenly she saw the malice in the woman. It frightened her. Rising hastily, regardless of her nakedness, she took up the rich cloth, the diaphanous bodice. The flimsy material was as a whisper between her fingers. She coloured as she felt the wetness between her thighs, then braced herself and stared coldly at the woman. I am a princess now, she thought. I will not be servile before one who is a servant. 'Leave the room!' she shouted.

The woman stepped back, startled.

'Now! Get out! Never show your face here again! None of you do I need. Ever!'

Carl Muller

KINGLY ACCEPTANCE

Duttha Gamani tossed in his sleep. The warmth of the night had been broken by a sudden fall of light rain and the change in the air made him stir. The cramps returned and he awoke to the squeezing sensation that hurt his ankles, his knees. He hated the cramps that made the flesh of his calves and his shins quiver and stretched his toes apart. He would leave his bed with an oath, try to press his feet on the cold floor, bend to rub the bands of flesh that rose over his ankles, rubbing them down with his thumbs.

With a small groan, he tried to stretch his legs, felt them tremble. The pain gripped him as he forced himself to rise, swing his legs to the left, feeling the slippers he trod on. Even the soles of his feet hurt. He sat, waiting for the cramps to subside.

Beyond the gauze blinds, the moon sulked behind a cloud with a silver-hemmed dress, and the trees of the Mahamega garden flashed back a million sparkles as an eerie radiance touched the drizzle and stayed upon their leaves. Slowly, the king eased back into bed. The cramps had died away, but he raised his legs carefully, placing his feet upon a pillow he had been told to use.

'Let your feet lie upon a raised pillow, lord,' the physician had said, 'for this will ease the strain upon them as you sleep.'

He closed his eyes. Then a voice spoke: 'In two days will the relics of the guide of the world be conveyed here.'

He jerked up, forgetting the pain at his knees as he swung his shoulders from left to right. There, where the carved door led to the passage and the balcony, where one copra torch burned in its scone, stood a figure with a large serpent hood poised over its head.

'Who—who be you?'

The voice hissed. 'I be Aravala. Deathless be I for my pride led me to use my Naga powers against the Holy Order. Now do I serve as the lowest of the low, a messenger of the devas who give me neither peace nor rest. I bring thee tidings that in two days will the relics of the Conqueror cometh hither. It is the wish of the devas that you observe on the morn a day of fasting.'

'You are of the Naga world, are you not—where the relics now are.'

'No. I am a Naga, as you see, but my torment is great. Captive I be—held for all time between life and death. Tired I be but have no rest. My eyes shed no tears, my hands wield no power, my mind thinks of that which I am bade to think. Thus must I suffer for my pride and my disdain for the truth...and yet, must you heed my words, for I say only what the devas give me leave to say. Tomorrow must all the land observe a day of fasting that all may be spiritually prepared. And on the next day must you observe a day of further fasting for that is when the relics will arrive and the blessings of the divine worlds pour as a flood upon this land.'

'So will we proclaim,' Duttha Gamani said. 'We—we thank thee. Is this truly what the devas wish, and will you remain for this great day, Naga lord?'

'Naga lord I be no more. I be but a servant for I was

the destroyer of the harvest and the destroyer of the happiness of men. For these faults do I now pay and in servility I wait the time of promise, for this too must end, and then will peace return to my bosom.'

'And this message—yes, we will proclaim the day of fasting at daybreak. It is glorious news you bring, for we await the coming of the relics with impatience.'

The figure seemed to smoke, and even as Duttha Gamani stared into the gloom, it became, he was certain, a huge serpent, losing all human form as the body transformed into a coiling sinewy band. He knew the searching stare of lidless eyes and as the smoke rolled away, heard the words in a sinuous whisper. 'Fasting and rejoicing...two days of fasting and rejoicing...' There was no sign of the ghostly visitor.

Rising, Duttha Gamani went to the door. The cloud cap had passed and the moon bathed the trees. The drizzle had ceased, but in the east, large masses of cloud rose, heavy and thick. He knew he could not try to sleep again. With a slight limp, he went to the bell rope. A dawn rain began to fall heavily as the palace officials assembled, asking each other why they had been summoned at so early an hour.

With the proclamation of the days of fasting, Duttha Gamani called for his palanquin and said to Tissa: 'Who among the brethren can tell of the Naga who calls himself Aravala? It was he who came to us in the early hours, bringing the instructions of the devas. What manner of Naga could he be?'

'Not of such a one have I heard. Do you wish to ask the monks, brother?'

'Aye, for no doubts have we of what he conveyed to us. Yet, he told of the abjectness of his existence but we did see the signs of much power in his being. A true Naga—serpent-hooded and human-headed—and he spoke as a man and went away as a great snake. Fasting and rejoicing... yes, those were his last words. And in our mind we heard yet another whisper. Seek no more greatness, it said, for even as the relics are enshrined will your greatness be known in all the worlds. We fear these words, brother. Is it that there is no more that we can achieve?'

Tissa shook his head. 'Methinks the hour and the strangeness of his coming has made you misunderstand. Surely did he say that this is the greatest thing you do. What can excel the enshrining of the holy relics? It is you who will take the urn in your hands, place it in the chamber, place it within the greatest edifice ever built. Think, brother, what greater act can a man perform and what greater act can you achieve? Be not troubled. It is your glory he surely spoke of.'

'Yes...you seem to have understood this Naga being... and yet, let us go to the monks. We must know more about this Aravala.'

The *Dipavamsa* says that the Third Buddhist Council took place in 247 BC. With the appearance of the Naga Aravala in the bedchamber of Duttha Gamani, it would be appropriate to trace back to the councils held after the death of the Buddha. The First Council was held at Rajagaha on the fourth month after the Buddha's passing away.[74] This was in the second Vassa month of Savana, the fifth month of the year which may be taken as June or July–August. This reckoning is based on the tradition that the Buddha died on the full moon day of the month of Vesakha—March or

April–May. The various chronicles agree that the originator of the First Council was Kasyapa.[75] The oldest account of this First Council is contained in the *Culavagga*.[76]

The Second Council, according to the *Culavamsa*, took place one hundred years after the Buddha's death. The chronicles agree that 700 monks took part and that it was held in the eleventh year of the reign of King Kalasoka, in 382 BC although the *Dipavamsa, Mahavamsa, Sasanavamsa* and the *Nikaya Sangrhaya* puts it in the tenth year. What was important about the Second Council held at Valikarama was that it was led by the thera Revata of Soreyya[77] who chastised the heretical monks who had sought to relax the orthodoxy of the Buddha's teachings. These heretical monks of the Vajji clan[78] had sought to relax the rules of the Dhamma and teach many things that were viewed to be unlawful. Ten of these listed in the *Culavamsa* are:

- *Singilonakappa*—The putting of salt in a horn vessel and carrying it around in order to season unsalted food that is offered.
- *Dvangulakappa*—The custom of taking the midday meal past the prescribed time as long as the sun's shadow had not passed the meridian by more than two finger-breadths.
- *Gamantarakappa*—The custom of going into the village after a meal and eating again if invited to do so.
- *Avasakappa*—The custom of holding the Uposatha feast separately by bhikkhus who live in the same district.
- *Anumatikappa*—Carrying out official acts by an incomplete charter on the assumption that such acts could be passed without a quorum and that the consent of absent bhikkhus could be obtained afterwards.
- *Acinnakappa*—The custom of doing something because of the preceptor's advice.

- *Amathitakappa—The practice of taking unchurned milk even after mealtime.*
- *Jalogikappa—The practice of drinking unfermented palm wine.*
- *Adasakam Nisidanam—The use of mats of unprescribed size to sit on which are also without a fringe.*
- *Jataruparajatam—The accepting of gold and silver.*

Naturally, the orthodox monks found these corruptions of the Dhamma reprehensible. The *Dipavamsa* tells us that the heretical monks refused to accept the decision of the Second Council and that instead, they held a separate council and made out a different redaction of the scriptures. They then formed a separate sect called Mahasamghika.

The Third Council was held under thera Mogaliputta in 247 BC at Pataliputta, the city of flowers.[79] It lasted, according to the *Mahavamsa,* for nine months, and, according to Fleet's reckoning,[80] began in the middle of January. At this Third Council, the canonical literature of the Dhamma and the Vinaya were completed in their essentials. The three councils were important in that they sought to eliminate tendencies inconsistent with the faith. The fact that the Second Council saw a division of the community of monks was not a serious rupture. The toleration that is characteristic of the Buddhists has not allowed the spawning of enmity. Indeed, the sects always mutually recognized each other and maintained relations. We have the words of the Buddha himself[81] concerning the future schools of Buddhism:

These schools will be the repositories of the diversified fruits of my Scriptures without priority or inferiority—just as the taste of sea water is everywhere the same—or as the twelve sons of one man, all honest and true, so will be the exposition of my doctrine advocated by these schools.

It was at the end of the Third Council that the thera Mogaliputta gave to the thera Majjhantika the task of carrying the doctrine into the Kashmiri region of Aravaladaha. This was one of the resolves of the council—that the faith be carried afar and in victorious passage through the entire eastern world.

The region of Aravaladaha was a fearsome one, for in it lay the dark lake of the same name, and in its depths did the Naga king of Kashmir find a secret passage to the Naga world. He was Aravala[82] who scorned the faith and would not have his Naga subjects embrace it. When Majjhantika was ordered to spread the doctrine, he knew that the task was a dangerous one. Aravala roared his displeasure. Returning from a night of revelry in the nether world, he had risen back and in serpent form from the lake to see a white blaze in the sky where Majjhantika hovered, showing himself to the Nagas who cowered in fear. It was the only way the monk could gain the attention of the people, display to them the potency of the truths he carried. Aravala stood, half-man, half-serpent, on the shores of the lake and, using his dark powers, caused lightning to lash out and the sky to become the colour of burnt oil. The clouds rushed upon the dazzling orb, inky and threatening, and hailstones flew with wicked intent and the thunder boomed and crackled and spat furiously.

Suspended in his orb of light, Majjhantika saw the mountains sway, and out of the clouds came long weaving tendrils that snaked around him, seeking with serpent venomousness, to crush the shining bubble of his defence. He floated calm-faced as the evil gibbered and hissed around him and watched as the Naga king cried out for his warriors. Slowly, he began to descend, stand upon the land among the people and made a gesture of peace. The light seemed to flow in all directions. It touched the prostrate Nagas and as it enfolded them, they rose and came towards him, their faces aglow.

With howls of rage, Aravala caused his spearsmen and archers to launch their missiles. These were of no avail. The light of redemption was everywhere. It coursed out even to the palace, moved ever on. Aravala assumed the form of a forbidding serpent-creature, the hood that sprouted from the back of his neck swaying viciously. With drawn sword he sped to where the monk stood. 'Is it that you defy me, the king of this land?' he spat. 'What brings you to my kingdom with your foul arts?'

Majjhantika cast tender eyes on him. 'Why do you hate the truth? Will you not let me tell of the truth?'

'Truth!' Aravala hissed. 'What truth do I need save that I am a king and this is my land and these are my people!'

'A sorry sort of truth is that, for the truth rests in a far deeper chamber than that of the obvious.'

The sword flashed and the blade sprang back in a shower of sparks as it bounced away from the encircling light. 'What magic is this,' he roared, 'that even the lightning does not find its mark!'

Duttha Gamani listened to the tale with eagerness. 'And it was this same tormented king that came to me...' The Maha Thera of the temple inclined his head. 'To us it is sad to hear of his visit, sire, for long had we hoped that he had found peace. But it is now certain that he works out the ages of his sentence. The thera Majjhantika, with loving calm, won him over and Aravala accepted the faith, but he has to pay for his misdeeds. But he did not allow himself to be possessed by anger and no more poured his wrath upon his people. Oh, he was given to such rages, sire, that he loved no one and in his evil moods would bring hail to destroy the crops and the harvests. And he embraced the faith, and all his people—84,000 in number. The thera exhorted him to let no anger rise as of old and he humbled himself and no more were the people, the crops, the harvests harmed. He learned how all beings love their happiness and that he must cherish love for all, even his lowliest subjects. He died a good, holy king, his passing mourned by all.'[83]

'But he is still serving his sentence,' Duttha Gamani exclaimed.

The monk nodded. 'What is time for the celestials? Their days are as our ages. But be assured, sire, King Aravala will earn peace, for his later days were filled with the truth.'

On the morning of the fast his uncle, Tissa, and the Brahmins had come, desirous to examine Devi, and Tissa had drawn Prince Saliya aside. 'It is not to heap scorn on you that your father sends the wise ones. Do you not see how much he loves you? He wishes to be told that this maid you have chosen has some signs of fortune. Understand, boy, that all this your father does to find a means of accepting the chandala. Would it not have been easier to banish her? Or enslave her? What would you do then? But he gives her instead all opportunity to reveal whether or not she is worthy of being your consort. Is that not overgenerous of him?'

Saliya had shrugged. 'Are you trying to tell me, Uncle, that my father would accept the chandala?'

It was Tissa's turn to shrug. 'How can I tell you that? But if he had no love for you, you would not remain here with the woman as you now do. You know not your father as I do. He has great capacity to forgive. I did him much wrong, nephew. I seized his elephant, his throne, wished his death...and when I lay trapped, beaten, he held his arms open, approached me, his enemy, and forgave me. Such a man is he, nephew. Doubt him not.'[84]

Saliya's expression had changed. 'Uncle, what is this burden that royal blood places on one? And see—the Brahmins wish to remain as long as they think it necessary to study her. They wish to ascertain her posture, the way she places her feet, the arch of her neck, the way her breasts hang and the manner of her hair at the line of her neck. Are there propitious signs to be found on the soles of her feet and the way her ears are shaped and how her fingers are? You have seen her. Is she not like a being divine? Is it her fault that she has been born a chandala?'

'Ah, there you err, nephew, for her birth is because of the manner of her previous life. This is what even the brethren have said to the king. You know how true this is. To be born a chandala—some grave fault must she have been guilty of before. It is this too that causes your father concern. Give the Brahmins leave to study her and let them carry their findings to your father. And take heart, nephew, for truly is she as gentle as she is beautiful. Her demeanour is that of a fawn. We have no doubt that her signs are good. Don't you see...she has already gained your love—the love of a prince. Is that in itself not fortunate of aspect?'

Carl Muller

Saliya smiled. 'Naught wiser have you said, uncle. When she is my queen, she will doubtless hold you in special favour.'

The Brahmins had sought to make their report after Duttha Gamani returned from the Maha Vihara. The palace was quiet and there was little sound of the serving women, and in the kitchens all was still. Duttha Gamani was glad to receive the wise ones. A day of religious fasting always seemed to move on leaden feet. Also, he was eager to hear their news.

The wise men had no reservations. 'O king, the young girl has all the auspicious signs which show that the possessor is fit to be the queen of a universal monarch.'

Duttha Gamani's eyes widened. 'And she is a chandala maid! Do we hear you say correct?'

'Chandala she is, sire, but indeed does the goddess of fortune, Sri Kanta, dwell within her. If any woman hath a beautiful head like the circle of a dark chatta, if her eyes be long and wide like the petals of the water lily, if her face glows like the lotus that lies in the sun, if her hands and feet are well rounded, then indeed is she favoured by the devas. Truly is she possessed of the sixty-four signs of female beauty, lord. That she has intoxicated the prince is of no real significance, for she is destined—and but a child in her ways the prince has known her and knitted himself to her. No worldliness did we see, no coldness, no hauteur. She is as an apsara, unconscious of her own beauty, a true queen among women. It amazes us to consider how she has grown, virginal, untouched, in the chandala quarter…but again, this has been her protection, for the men of the city often take a chandala maid even if only as a last resort. Again, in this do we see the workings of the fortunate signs, for we feel she has been preserved for the prince. It is as if the devas have led them to each other.'

Duttha Gamani marvelled. Could it be that such a maid had dwelt, had grown to womanhood unnoticed? He dismissed the Brahmins, conscious that no soft food or drink could he offer them. 'We will see this girl,' he said, turning to Tissa. 'Are even the wise ones made victim of her beauty? And what say you, brother?'

'She is what every king would seek. I think you should see her, but is it necessary that this should be done today?'

'Yes. Tomorrow is a day of great gladness. And know you that the prince must also attend the enshrinement. What if he brings the maid with him? That would be foolhardy of him if he has not our leave. It is best that he knows of our stance.'

'Agreed. Thousands enter the city. Thousands will stand around the Maha Thupa. The prince cannot stand together with a chandala. That would be unthinkable, brother.'

The Puranas give us an idea of the propitious signs that the Brahmins looked for in a woman, and there is little doubt that they found them all in Asokamala Devi—all that was auspicious. Their assessment would have also included palmistry and they would have even wished the girl to frown that they may see the way the lines formed on her forehead. The *Garuda Purana* tells us of what was looked for: curling locks, a round face, a deep navel. The skin must be of a golden glow and unblemished, and the hands soft, reddish, and without perspiration. Even the lines of the palm must be red, for lines that are dark or bluish reveal that the person is unchaste. As the Purana says:

> The auspicious signs of women are cool and high breasts, copper-coloured nails, beautiful feet, marks of fish, goad, lotus, discus or ploughshare on the soles and palms which

do not perspire, beautiful hips without hairs, thighs like the trunk of an elephant, most excellent and capacious, buttocks like a fig leaf, spacious and deep navel and chest and breast shorn of hairs.

Her knee joints must be fleshy and dimpled, her nipples not very high and her well-rounded and fleshy arms must be long and well-formed. Her fingers must be straight and her lips red, smiling and tender. Her teeth must be sharp and even, and there must be no blemish on her tongue. The ears must be flat against the head, quite spear-like, the cheeks well-formed and the nose straight with a beautiful tip and small nostrils. Her eyes must be like lotus petals with a little curve at the corners and the forehead elevated. Also the shape of the head to be like a dark parasol. This is the accepted sign of royalty, auspiciousness and riches.

All in all, it is thought that a woman who has an even nose and displays the virtues of mercy and simplicity is always the most fortunate. Her eyebrows must not be very thick, and great good attends the woman who has a line on her palm that rises from the wrist and goes to the base of the middle finger. Even her hips must not be too high, for it has been said that a woman with high hips kills her husband!

No, there was no blemish whatsoever in Asokamala Devi. She was made to be the rarest of women, of exceeding loveliness, made to be a queen. And she had given herself to Saliya, scarcely knowing that she was moving to fulfil the promise of her own self.

It was with some reluctance that Saliya rode to the palace. The king had desired that he present himself together with the chandala maid, and he was angered to be told that

Asokamala Devi would be conveyed in a closed palanquin and with scant ceremony. 'Why? Is she a contamination that she be borne hence so secretively? May she not ride with me as she did when I bore her into the city?'

The chief minister raised a soothing hand. 'Be not troubled, for that is what thy father and the council wishes. The people are distressed and this is a day of fasting too. Many have raised voices of concern, even protest. Surely it is wise that she be borne to the palace in this manner. And when the king has seen her and has decided, there will be no need of such secrecy any more.'

Saliya gave in. 'It will be as our father wishes, but I know that my princess will feel the slight.'

'I think not, O prince. She knows her station, does she not? Her people have always been slighted. Surely she understands that she goes thus to stand before the king. What chandala in all this land has been so honoured?'

As they rode to the palace, Saliya could not help thinking of the chief minister's last remark. Suddenly he knew a great love for his father. 'What other king indeed,' he muttered and realized that he could not come up to the sick man's shoulders. When he stood before Duttha Gamani, his first words were: 'O king, in love and devotion I ask this of you. Let my uncle, the king of the south, sit upon this throne. It is not for me to succeed thee, for I have cast my lot with the outcaste and have found my greatest happiness there.'

Duttha Gamani looked sadly at the youth. 'Our son,' he said after a long minute of silence. 'As a boy you have been so different, a lover of the arts and with the soul of a maid. It is that we have been remiss in your upbringing, and yet did our mother love you deeply and it was she who asked that you be viceroy…but we will not stand in your way. We will look upon this maiden of your choice and all that we say or do not say will not really matter, will it? But know you, our son, that always do you have our love. At this our age, what does pride matter? You have our leave to take your future into your own hands and that of the one you love, and we seek no more loyalty of prince to king—only that of a son to a father. Yes, our brother Tissa shall be king and to him will we confer the sovereignty of all the land...ah, do we not hear the handbells of the women. They announce the coming of your princess. Go, bring her hither.'

Tissa ran a hand on his beard. He wanted to say so much, but Duttha Gamani said, 'Sons have you, my brother. Fortunate indeed are you, for they will keep the south secure and even the eastern and western coasts. Tomorrow will we proclaim you our successor. Think you that this is the work of the devas. Our son would have caused many social dissensions for who would abide a chandala as a royal consort? Even the council is at odds and who can say what the future will hold?'

'Our brother speaks true, and yet, when you look upon this woman you will you know the full extent of the prince's love. She is as divine and such beauty inflames all.'

Duttha Gamani looked at Devi and was filled with joy. 'Are you the fortunate one whom our son calls Asokamala Devi?' he asked.

The girl bowed. 'It is so, O lord.'

'Come closer, fair one. Sit you here at our knee. Know you that we have let ourselves become estranged from our son and did not know of such treasure as he has found. No queen will you be, Asokamala Devi, but gladly do we give you our son, for the Brahmins tell of your goodliness and our brother proclaims your beauty. Now do our old eyes see how real is your worth...for we say to you—and to you, Saliya—come, sit ye at our right knee...in this world, if a man finds a bezoar stone in the rotting carcase of a bull, will he keep the stone even if the carcase is spoilt and must be thrown away? What does it matter to which family one is born? The virtuous one is always the superior. We will build a great palace in the north where you may live and we will let it be known throughout the land that you will remain as a sub-ruler of that district you are given and where you will rule righteously and protect your territory and follow the teachings of the Buddha...aye, even after our death. Come then, our son. Take our hand in acceptance and our other hand in sign of acceptance of your woman.'

'Father, do we return in the order in which we came?'

Duttha Gamani smiled. 'No, for no such need will there be. An open chariot will take you, and your woman will sit beside you, and an escort of standard-bearers will ride with you.' He turned to Devi. 'No Asoka flowers do you wear, but in this chest will you find garlands of rubies as red as the flowers you love. Wear one upon your breasts as you leave.'

'And tomorrow. Father...what of her?'

'She must attend, and a special place will we provide, and an escort of Naga maidens will wait on her. Yet will you come separately, for beside us must you be.'

Saliya bowed. He could not question the decision and saw its merit.

There were few citizens to remark on their passage back. The day of fasting kept many indoors. In the late morning light the rubies flashed round Asokamala Devi's neck and the largest of them between her breasts was like a huge scarlet eye.

THE BELLY OF THE SERPENT

Night clenched its fingers over Anuradhapura. From all points dark clouds rolled over the fields, the ghostly roads, the frowning jungles. Even the lamps that made their orange-yellow slide shows in the windows could only make half-hearted forays into the darkness. In the Maha Vihara, the monks squatted, hands pressed together, and their litany was soft and leaden

Duttha Gamani stood, wondering at the blackness. Even the white cupola of the great thupa, around which hundreds of torches had been placed, seemed to have dissolved in the shadows of mountainous clouds that held the sky, even the moon prisoner. The air was still, the heat fearsome, and he had no mind to even make conversation with his brother who stood with him. Tissa was barebodied, as was the king, and there was a line of sweat at the edge of his headwrap.

'Who can sleep in this heat,' Tissa grumbled. 'Never have I known a darker night.'

'Or a hotter. It is as if we are in some airless cave, and we see no lights of any number at the Maha Thupa. Did we not order many torches?'

'Yes, brother, and I saw them lit. They burn low tonight. There is no breeze to fan the flames.'

'Hmm...you may be right.'

They stood in silence.

At the Maha Vihara, the thera Indagutta rose, motioned to the monks. 'It is not right that we should go forth in the dark hours, so we shall choose a point where we hold the Maha Thupa in sight. The outer corridors. There must we meditate until I say that all is well. Think upon the darkness, the hot belly of the serpent and will that light invade it. Think upon the journey that one of us take through foetid paths that are surrounded with moving hoops of bone, now widening, now constricting. Let your thoughts push back this cage, enlarge it, make the dark way easy for the one who lies with us as if in death. It is now that he needs our help. Let us go to the western corridor. Keep your eyes, your minds on the dagaba and let not the darkness befuddle you.'

They filed out. In his cell, feeling neither the heat nor aware of the black caul that stretched over the city, the young arahat Sonuttara lay as in death. His astral form was far away, deep in the earth, preparing to bring back the treasure he sought.

Duttha Gamani was tired. He turned, as if to retire to his chamber, then moved again to look at the colossal thupa. He gave a cry. 'What is it! See, Tissa—tell us we are not dreaming!'

'No,' said Tissa huskily, 'but what is it...like hoops of ivory, and they seem to encase the thupa...'

'Is it—is it that the relics have arrived?'

'But who could tell us. Do we send a message to the monks?'

Duttha Gamani's hands shook. 'It is so late...but yes, they must be told. But surely they also see what we see...'

It was an awesome sight. The blanketing clouds seemed

Carl Muller

to have dropped curtains of black over the thupa. All around it and even at edges of the park lay a sea of darkness—impenetrable darkness. It seemed to have been poured on, an inky sea where no waves rose. Out of the immense cloud roof had come questing fingers of a mottled tarnished white: fingers of the colour of ancient bone, fingers that curled and curved and glowed unreally as they touched the ground, caging the dagaba.

'It's—it's—what *is* it?' Duttha Gamani exclaimed. He was trembling. 'It is as if some giant has brought down a hand and fingers of bone wish to clutch at the thupa. Quickly, Tissa, rouse somebody, anybody...we must alert the monks, send word to the Maha Thera.'

Thera Indagutta raised his hands. 'The belly of the serpent,' he whispered. 'It is a time so critical, O monks. Let your every thought go forth to the holy Sonuttara, give to him assurance of his success.'

When the chamberlain stumbled up to the corridor with a torch-bearer to guide him, Indagutta said he knew of the vision and that the king need not be alarmed. 'I will send back one of the brethren with you. Tell the king that this heat will not allow the night's sleep. Let those of the palace assemble in the main hall that they may all remain upon the cooler stone floor and then will they be led in prayer. Keep the holy relics foremost in all minds for they need to be wrested away from the world of the serpent men, drawn from the maw of the Naga world. But assure the king that what we have set out to do will be done.'

Kala Naga did not like what he saw, and yet, he eyed the young monk warily. There was no impatience of manner—and but a boy! Just a messenger sent from above. Yet there was no shrinking in his voice. Was it that he had a force that awaited his signal? He saw Vasuladatta, his nephew, edging up. 'What is this you demand?' he roared, and his breath was as an outpouring of crushed forest leaves. 'You ask that I give up to you what the devas had miraculously placed at the door to my world! Do you then also defy the celestial ones?'

'That is not a question that merits an answer, for it is known that the relics have been sent here for a short time only. They are destined for a resting place in the world above.'

'And how short do you say is this time that has been given?'

'When I have taken the casket and have gone, you may count the hours and know how short a time it is.'

Vasuladatta seemed to blur in the light of the crystal lamps. His voice was an angry hiss. 'The serpent beings keep what is given to them! And what power is greater than that of the Nagas?'

Before Sonuttara's eyes he transformed himself. The large hood seemed to swell, the head disappeared into the serpent's throat and the body elongated, dissolving into the coils of a monstrous serpent.

Kala Naga rose. 'Secure the casket, nephew! Hold it within you that none may take it!'

With a flaming hissing, the serpent moved, flowing like a jet of dark onyx and amber as it swept out of the chamber. Kala Naga laughed. 'You stare? That is the greatest of my serpent warriors. His powers are talked of even in the abodes of the devas.'

Sonuttara nodded. 'Yes. He will now take what I have come for. He will go, even to the centre of the world systems, and he will do so because he fears that I will succeed. Is that not so?'

'Fear you? Who fears one with shaven head and the ill-fitting robes of a penitent? Is it that we must fear you even after we have received you as our guest?'

'I do not ask to be thy guest. I come to take what must belong to the Great Thupa of the blessed island, and that is what I must do.'

'Do so, then, if you must, and we will be kind and comfort thee in thy failure.'

'Your warrior nephew streams away. He has swallowed the urn, clutches it within his belly. He thinks that there it will be safe.'

'I think you speak with little reason. Come, let us show you where the relics are held.'

Sonuttara allowed himself a small twitch of his lips. His senses had told him all he wished to know. He had seen in his mind how the great serpent had taken the urn and with a surging of supernatural power, driven his way into the floor, coursed through the nether regions to emerge through a long crevice on the flanks of Mount Sineru.[85] There did Vasuladatta coil himself, at the foot of the cloud-capped mountain over which the devas resided.

He grew to monstrous size.[86] Yet, the serpent being was not satisfied. The *Mahavamsa* says:

He created many thousand heads with puffed-up hoods,
he belched forth, as he lay there, smoke and fire. When
he then had created many thousand snakes like to himself,
he made them lie about him in a circle.

On the holy mountain, the devas gathered to watch, while serpent gods rose from the belly of the earth. They knew that there would be combat. The young ascetic would surely come to claim the relics. How would he overcome such a Naga force?

In the Naga kingdom, Sonuttara apparently showed no concern, not even when Kala Naga said, 'Why do you remain here with that strange look in your eyes? There are no relics here.'

'Yes, that I know, for they have been taken hence.'

'Come you then. You shall satisfy yourself.'

They went to the temple. There, leading to the repository, were the marble steps and there did Kala Naga pause. 'See you, O bhikkhu, look around. Do you not see how well we give honour to the sacred relics? See how this temple is adorned with many gems and how nobly it is built. And see you this carved stone slab.' He pointed to an exquisitely carved half-moon tablet with its rings of gracefully executed ornaments. 'All the jewels in all of your Lanka will not pay for work such as this. And all this did the Nagas do in honour of the treasure sent to us. Tell me, bhikkhu, do you come to take from this place of highest honour, the relics to a place of lesser honour?'

Sonuttara's eyes flashed. For the first time he showed his mettle. 'I grow tired of this prevarication, Kala Naga. You speak to me of value, of your priceless adornments. You boast of the riches you fill this temple with, but do these rich trappings signify the understanding of the *ariyasaccani*?[87] It is now doubly so that I insist, for I see no acceptance of the noble truths among you Nagas. It is indeed fitting that I bear away the relics to where understanding and truth prevail. Know, O King, that the tathagathas are born for deliverance from *samsara*—that endless procession of life and death. Thereon is the Buddha intent. What does it profit even your immortal journey if it be only to fill your days with riches and power? As you wield your whip now, who will belabour you with a cudgel when your age ends? You seek not the truth although in times past you were a lover of the truth. The relics cannot remain in this world of high honour, as you say. I have come to bear them away, for it is passing midnight and growing closer to the dawn time in the island of the truth, and it is on this very day that the king will set about enshrining the relics.' His voice became a whiplash. 'Quickly then! Give me the relics.'

Kala Naga paled. 'Take the urn then. If you can see the relics, take them.'

'And do you, as king of the Nagas, say that I can remove the relics?'

'Did I not say so? If you can see them, take them.'

'And you are certain that this you permit me to do?'

'What is it that ails you, venerable one? Did I not say that you can take the relics and go?'

Sonuttara gave a small bow. 'I thank you, Kala Naga. The monks of the Buddha thank you and the great king of Lanka, whose throne is the seat of the lion, thanks you.' With a flash blinding light Sonuttara changed into a formless spirit of pure energy. Like an arrow, he pulsed, invisible, thrusting out with incredible power, reaching in a split second the growling waters, rising out of them to sweep through the upper world. Unseen, he reached the gathering of serpents, the congregation of devas, the writhing guardians who hissed and roared around the monstrous form of Vasuladatta.

The giant serpent being, issuing sulphurous fumes from its nostrils, did not see or know of the ribbon of energy that thrust itself into its mouth—the long arm of the invisible being that hovered outside the circle of snakes. Vasuladatta felt the urn move strangely in his belly and opened his mouth to suck in air. Swiftly the relics were drawn up his throat and an explosion of light blinded him as, open-mouthed, he flailed about. On the mountain, the devas saw the extraction of the urn and knew that it would be borne as swiftly away.

'Stay, holy one,' called the deva Samtusita, 'for we come with thee.'

'And all of us,' called the deva Suyama, in a thin fluting voice.

Far down the slopes, Sonuttara materialized. 'Do the celestial ones travel with me?' he asked, taking the casket from the wraps of his robe. 'Return I must the way I came, and I must now travel fast.'

'We will bear you as swiftly and in as short a time as you wish, for we come with you. Hold you up the urn that you have taken from the belly of the serpent so that we may pay worship to it, for we have much to offer in so doing.'

It was but the time of a fleeting thought. The dawn had just begun to struggle through the massy clouds. Suddenly, the coverlet of black paled, smoked away and the cupped-finger cage of ivoried bone that seemed to hold the Great Thupa prisoner, disappeared.

In the corridor, Indagutta rose with a growing excitement. 'Quick,' he told the monks. 'We must go to the cell of Sonuttara. See, no more is there the darkness and the air is cool and the belly bones of the serpent have disappeared. Yes, the clouds have begun to roll away. The time of crisis is over. Let us hasten.'

They found Sonuttara where he lay and the young monk's eyes were open, and beside him, on a pile of saffron wraps, stood the jewelled urn. The young ascetic said, 'I thirst.' 'Do not try to rise. Lie you yet, for you are

Carl Muller

drained and need time to recover. You have done well...
but what is that music I hear?'

'Music? But I am alone...no, stay. I did not return alone.
The devas bore me back, even through the mountains of
cloud. I may not have been able to return unaided for I
cast aside my mock form to enter the serpent's belly. When
I materialized I was weak, much weakened.'

Indagutta took up the urn lovingly. 'Now will all good
things come to be. Water will you have and some gruel
when you can sit up. But rest you must. You have done
all that was wished of you.' He then hurried out to send
a message of glad tidings to the palace.

The *Mahavamsa* gives us a detailed account of the
enshrining of the relics. We are told of the coming of the
gods and how a beautiful pavilion was raised upon the spot
where Sonuttara had pierced the earth. There did the god
Sakka place a jewelled throne upon which the relics were
placed. Over the throne Brahma raised a parasol. Samtusita
waved a yak-tail whisk and Suyama a jewelled fan. Sakka
blessed the spot with water from a large shell. The four
guardians of the world, the Lokapalas, also came, swords
in their hands. Thirty-three other gods brought baskets
of flowers, the *Paricchattaka* flowers which only bloom in
the Tavatimsa heaven. Thirty-two celestial maidens carried
lamps and twenty-eight Yakkha chieftains stood guard. Even
as the deva Pancasikha played his lute and Timbaru set
up a stage for dancing and song,[88] a certain consternation
spread as hordes of Nagas appeared.

They were led by Kala Naga. The king had been at first
angry, then full of grief. When Sonuttara disappeared he

had laughed. 'The bhikkhu has gone. We have deceived him, for how could he take relics that are not here?' He had laughed again as he instructed his chieftains to recall his nephew. 'Let him return, for now the relics are surely ours.'

Vasuladatta had known that something was amiss. He could not be sure but somehow he feared that the urn was no more in his belly. And yet, if it were and he should take human form, it would surely burst through his stomach, killing him. He had called upon the Naga gods of the mountain and had been told that many devas had gone with an ascetic who carried an urn in the folds of his robe. With a cry, Vasuladatta had sped back. When he had stood before Kala Naga in his human form, he had little to say.

Kala Naga could hardly believe that his nephew had lost the urn. 'And I said to the monk—thrice I said to him that he may take the urn! We have been betrayed! That bhikkhu had power we knew not of. Did you not see him as he approached?'

'I saw nothing.'

'But from within you! How could he reach into you and you not know of it?'

Vasuladatta bowed his head. 'I felt—I felt my belly heave, O uncle, and then there was great light and an emptiness. But the gods saw and said no word. Is it that our Naga gods also wished that we surrender that which was given us?'

Kala Naga had been filled with grief. 'This is a dark day!' he cried aloud and many fell to the floor to lament with him.

Thera Indagutta stood in the way of the Naga's approach. 'Why have you come, King Maha Kala?'

'These are my people. See how woeful they be. And I, their king, weep with them and for them. Is the worship of the relics of the Master only to henceforth be for the people of this island? Is it that after we received them and did much honour, we are now deprived of what was miraculously ours?'

'And yet, O Maha Kala, did you do honour to the lord of the world when you consigned his holy relics to the belly of the serpent? Even here did we see the signs of this mishandling. Here, where the relics are to be rightfully enshrined, was a field of darkness and all around were the ribs of the snake. Thus did we know of the great disrespect you had shown. Know you that the relics were to remain in your world for but a short time. Thus was it said even as the tathagatha lay dying. Knew you not of this?'

The serpent king lowered his eyes. 'We own our fault, venerable one, but that does not ease our grief.'

Indagutta's face softened. 'And do you now come to reclaim the relics or to pay obeisance to them?'

'We come to tell you of our sorrow...and to worship as we worshipped in the temple we raised for the urn. Deny us not, venerable one, for gladly will we remain here if only to worship that which is so treasured by gods and men.'

'Your words gladden me, Naga king. I will speak with the council of monks and with the king, and a small part of the relics will we give to you to take back to your world that your temple will not be empty.'

Kala Naga was overjoyed. He led his people to the pavilion and they were loud in their devotions. All around, assembled in the five directions[89] bhikkhus chanted, for it was time for the arrival of the king.

A great golden casket had been prepared—a casket Duttha Gamani bore on his head as he approached. It was early evening, the evening of a full moon day. Tissa assisted his brother to enter the chariot and stand under the white umbrella of dominion. Four white horses drew the chariot, stepping delicately along at a measured pace. Tissa stood beside his brother, and behind, in an equally magnificent chariot rode Saliya, resplendent in his silken dress of state.

The road to the Maha Vihara was decorated with flowers, banners and torches, and even as they approached the pavilion, accompanied by bands of singers and musicians and dancers, tended by a guard of warriors and a large body of troops, the devas rained down heavenly perfumes. All around the pavilion, a guard of Yakkha and Naga lords held copper umbrellas. These had been ordered by Indagutta who knew that copper would ward off the influence of the arch-demon Mara.

Duttha Gamani was amazed. Truly were the devas all around. He listened to the celestial music, knew the heavy fall of perfumed rain, saw the celestial parasol over the relics, the exquisite pavilion, felt the scented breeze on his face. 'Are not the Brahma gods all around us?' he said, and Tissa nodded dumbly. Stepping down from his chariot, Saliya felt he had stepped into a deva world. Entranced, he looked not for Devi who was being escorted to a special place at the fringes of the great thupa.

'Who am I but a man in the garments of a king,' Duttha Gamani said. 'There is the true king of this land.'

Tissa was startled. 'My brother, what mean you?'

'We are kings, yes...but can we bring the gods down to walk this land? Who can bless this land as the holy relics can? There, Tissa, there in that urn is the passion of the centuries. There lies the true king of Lanka.'

Laying the relics in the golden casket, he placed it on his

head and walked to the thupa. The monks surrounded him, chanting their songs of jubilation. Three times, keeping left, he circumnavigated the huge stupa, then climbed the steps of the terraces at the east. At the stone steps leading to the relic chamber, he stopped, placed the casket on the throne of offerings and raised his hands.

'To the master of the world, to the teacher who bears the threefold parasol, the parasol of the heavenly host, the canopy of mortals and the canopy of eternal emancipation…thrice over do we now declare, thrice over do we dedicate, thrice over do we entrust this land to the redeemer of the world, thrice over do we consecrate our kingly rank…'

All around, from thousands of throats rose the joyous salutation: *'Saadhu, Saadhu,'* and around Duttha Gamani there seemed as if a light shimmered. Taking up the casket once more and placing it upon his head, he turned to face the monks, the people, his son, his brother. 'Behold thy king,' he said. 'From this day forth, these sacred relics hold kingship over Lanka.' He entered the relic chamber, deposited the casket on the altar.

It was the time for the goblets and basins, the jars of aromatic unctions. Duttha Gamani stood patiently while his feet and hands were bathed in the fragrant water and anointed with sweet pastes. His eyes sought Indagutta's as if to ask a question, but the monk looked at him impassively. Indagutta would take no part in the rest of the proceedings. He had read, in the soft aura that surrounded the king, that this was the king's day…the day of heavenly reward, as it were, for the years of labour and unremitting toil. Whatever the king thought fit would he do and could do.

Duttha Gamani moved as if in a dream. With steady hands, he opened the casket and bowed over it in profound reverence. Then, when the inner casket lay open, the relics exposed to view, he drew a sharp breath and his voice shook. 'If it be destined that these relics should permanently repose anywhere...and if it should be destined that that these relics should be enshrined here, where they will remain, providing a refuge of salvation for the people of this land and of all the world, may these relics take the form of the divine teacher...may these relics cause to appear as the wonder of the ages, seated upon the throne of Buddhahood...may this be a sign for all the land...' He turned, said to Indagutta, 'Let the Naga king Maha Kala come hither.'

Tissa asked at the entrance: 'Why seeks he the Naga?'

Indagutta made no answer, even as he signalled to Kala Naga to enter the chamber. He then said: 'Thy brother remembers all. What he now does and says comes not from himself alone but because a divinity has possessed him. Now he holds the memory of the times before, yes, even to the times of the arahat Mahinda's father, the great Asoka.'

'But what...'

'Softy, O King. Watch, and all will be known.'

Kala Naga stood as though he was a graven image. He, the immortal of wondrous might, had beheld four Buddhas who had lived through the ages.

Centuries ago, he had sat, dressed in chains of gold, before Emperor Asoka of Pataliputta. There stood the great thera, Mogaliputta Tissa and there were the tall jars which contained the water drawn from the Anotatta Lake.

The emperor had received him with all honour. 'You, O Maha Kala, have this wondrous gift. Hark you, for even as the theras say there are eighty-four thousand sections of the dhamma, each one of them have we decided to honour with a vihara. Ninety-six kotis of money have we deposited in eighty-four thousand towns. Here, in our capital have we begun to build the Asokarama.[90]

'Know you then, Maha Kala, that in all the viharas of the world would there be needed the image of the great sage…Tell us, is it not true that even when a disciple of the Buddha wished to make such an image and could not do so as accurately as he wished, the Buddha told him to trace his shadow on the groud and use that? Thus were the proportions arrived at.[91] Now, O Maha Kala, do we ask that you create for us the bodily form of the omniscient great sage. Do so that we may take all detail of form. How can we set our sculptors to work if the details remain hidden from us; for just as the master set rolling the wheel of the true doctrine, do we need his likeness that the wheel roll throughout this land, in all the eighty-four thousand towns where his image shall be.'

Maha Kala had assented. Using his extraordinary powers, he had created a beauteous figure of the Buddha. On it were the thirty-two great signs and eighty lesser signs of the Buddha.[92] Asoka had been filled with joy at the sight and had exclaimed: 'Even such is the image created by Maha Kala—nay, then what would have been the real form of the tathagatha like?'

Somehow, the ancient memory of Maha Kala's particular role had arisen, unbid, in Duttha Gamani's mind. He said, 'Tell us, O King of the Nagas, if what you will now see is just as you caused Emperor Asoka to see.'

Kala Naga stood before the king. He knew that somehow, his powers seemed to lie in the hands of this aged king who stood within an aura of softest light.

Then inexplicably, the casket rose in the air, floating over their heads.

ENSHRINEMENT AND THE ROAD TO IMMORTALITY

THE *SARIPUTRA* SAYS THAT IMAGES OF THE BUDDHA MAY BE MADE of gold, copper, clay, stone, wood, brick and lime. Silver, brass, bronze and ivory have also been used, as well as alabaster and crystal. As often as not there were 'groups' as we see in many temples in Sri Lanka. Even King Duttha Gamani has been so honoured where, in the Ridi Vihara[93] in Kurunegala[94] a later king ordered a great sleeping image of the Buddha, as well as others seated and standing, made with fine brick, mortar and clay. At the foot of this sleeping image we also have images of the Buddha's disciple, Ananda, the Bodhisatva Metteiya, the god Natha and King Duttha Gamani.

What are interesting are the units of measurement of the craftsmen. There is no mention in the *Sariputra* of the ordinary architect's cubit,[95] the foot[96] and the span.[97] Instead, we have an *angala*.[98] However, Coomaraswamy[99] says the angala was not merely a fixed measure and could also be referred to as a unit, as the instructions are intended to provide for all sizes of images. The other unit is the *mukha*[100]—13½ inches: the measurement from the base of the hair on the forehead to the chin.

Some of the instructions in the *Sariputra* will be of interest. There are *alpa*,[101] *adhama*,[102] *madhyama*,[103] *uttama*[104] and *maha*[105] images. No images of gold or other metal should be cast hollow within. The making of hollow images will result, before long, in the loss of wife or wealth and lead to quarrels or famine. Kings will begin to fear their enemies and there will be many incidents that will delay the making of the image. The joints of images of wood and stone must be positioned exactly. Long life is assured those who do so. If not, if even a deviation of half an inch is made, the result is loss of wealth and death.

The length of the face is 13½ inches and the *usnisha*[106] is equal to eight *yarva*.[107] This usnisha or 'bump of wisdom' is said to represent the extra-cranial capacity of the Buddha, though there are some who say that it symbolizes the thatch of hair that remained after the Buddha cut off his hair in his act of renunciation. Indian legends have it that the usnisha bulge is also a relic kept in a stupa in Bihar.

However, scholars have pointed to the Bactrian Greek statues of the Buddha in Gandhara as the forerunners of the depiction of the extra-cranial bump. And yet, Duttha Gamani needed to know, even in this hour of his greatest spirituality, whether all the labours of his craftsmen were without blemish, especially in the astonishing work done in the adornment of the relic chamber. Also, he had now given the relics kingship—but would it be said in later times that there, in the Maha Thupa, lies entombed the king of Lanka? The people must see this king, fall prostrate before him, know the glory of his presence and spread the joyous news. Songs must be written and verses sung, and in music, literature, art and history must it be accepted that the Sakyamuni of royal birth is the monarch of the world, and here is one of his abodes.

The casket floated even up to the roof and then descended to shoulder level. Suddenly the rich walls of fat-coloured stone seemed to pulse with light, and streaks of the purest amber, vermillion and puce danced over the high altar, turning their shafts to make the golden throne burst into a million points of colour. A light, as from an immense lantern, held the casket and from all around came the aroma of the rarest perfumes.

Slowly the relics rose—flakes of bone, lengths, curves, pieces smooth, jagged, crenellated. Tissa made an instinctive step forward while outside thousands fell to their knees, bathed in an ethereal blue that seemed to come from the chamber. The monks crouched, their faces illumined and in one tremendous voice, sang the salutation to the Buddha:

Iti'pi so Bhagava: Araham Samma-sambuddho,
Vijjacararana-sampanno, Sugato Loka-vedu,
Anuttaro punsadamma Sarathi, Sattha deva-manussanam,
Buddho Bhagava'ti
Namo tassa Samma-Sambuddhassa!
Ye ca Buddha atita ca—Ye ca Buddha anagata,
Pacuppana ca ye Buddha—Aham vandami sabbada
N'atthi me saanam annam—Buddho me sarana varam!
Etena sacca—vajjena—Hotu me jaya-mangalam!
Uttamangena vande'ham—Padapamsu var'uttamam,
Buddhe yo khalito doso—Buddho khamatu tam mamatri
Buddham jivita—pariyantam Saranam gacchami.

Such indeed is the Blessed One, Exalted, Omniscient, Endowed with knowledge and virtue, Auspicious, Knower

Carl Muller

of Worlds, a Guide incomparable for the training of individuals, Teacher of Gods and Men, Enlightened and Holy.

Homage to that Enlightened One!
The Buddhas of the ages past,
The Buddhas that are yet to come,
The Buddhas of the present age,
Lowly, I each day adore!
No other refuge do I seek,
Buddha is my matchless refuge;
By might of truth in these my words,
May joyous victory be mine!
With my brow I humbly worship,
The blest dust on His Holy Feet;
If Buddha I have wronged in aught,
May I not do it e'er again.
To life's end, my refuge is the Buddha.

Slowly the relics took form. They moved into place to become first a sketchy figure and then, as if at a signal, the luminosity was cut away and in its place a radiant figure appeared. Duttha Gamani and Kala Naga fell to their knees, bending over that their faces met the cold stone. Thera Indagutta raised his hand and moved to take Tissa by the arm. They stepped out of the doorway where, with Saliya, they bowed low. It was certain that the devas moved in accord, for around the prostrate kings rose the scent of flowers, camphor, perfume and aromatic smoke. The form of the Buddha gleamed with the greater and lesser signs and somehow, this same form also hovered above the terraces, glowing richly against the stupa, to be seen by all.

The *Mahavamsa* tells us that with this miracle of double appearance, twelve kotis of devas and men attained arahatship and none could count the people who attained the three levels of salvation. This miracle had been performed by the Buddha repeatedly. The same was wrought before the laying of relics within the thupa of the Bodhi tree. Again, there is the miracle performed at Savitthi to refute the heretical teachers. Many such miracles also caused the appearance of phenomena of opposite character in pairs, such as fire and water.

All around the great thupa, the people of Anuradhapura, indeed almost all of Lanka—for many had gathered from every part of the island and great numbers had come from India and other lands—saw that which they had never before been privileged to see. There, within the repository, was the Buddha; there beside the dagaba was the Buddha...and yet those who stood in crowded ranks around the thupa saw the Master too. Many sobbed at the sheer beauty of the figure, the face full of compassion, a tenderness that no human could register. Women beat their hands on their breasts, their eyes streaming...and far away, on the red-sand bund of the Tissa Wewa, a shadowy form arose, soared over the trees and hovered unseen. It was that of a woman, and none among the crowd saw her for they could not tear their eyes away from the form of the Master. With a catch of joy in her breath, Vihara Maha Devi bowed with hands clasped, then slowly faded back into the shadows of the rain trees, and melted upon the waters.

Slowly the music of the devas faded, and Duttha Gamani raised his head to see the form dissolve, the relics return to the casket. He rose, and so did the Naga king who said, his voice almost breaking, 'That these relics were taken from my world, even when I opposed such an act, now tells me how ill-favouredly I behaved. And yet have I been rewarded. Know you that I sought to retain the urn because of my great love for the Master. Is it that that has earned me such favour?'

'We cannot say, but surely do you now know that this is the true repository as was told by the Buddha himself.'

'That I now know. It is now left that we complete the ceremony.'

Duttha Gamani nodded. He beckoned to Tissa. 'Come, brother, for we will enthrone the casket.'

Tissa placed the casket on the king's head and once again a solemn procession was conducted around the chamber. Yet, on the jewelled throne, the casket seemed to lose its lustre. 'No,' he thought, 'this should not be.' He was confused. And why had he suddenly felt his mother's presence? She seemed to be close, warm against him and yet, when the apparition had faded, she had gone too. He told Tissa, 'Did you not know that our mother was also here?'

Tissa shook his head. 'We must now close the chamber, brother, for it grows late and before long it will be night. Think of the people. Many have bided here since the early hours.'

'Yes, we think of the people. Always must we think of them.' He called for water.

'What is it?' asked Tissa, 'Is there need for self-purification once again?'

'It is for our people, brother. Direct you the order of the purification.'

Again was he washed in perfumed water and his body anointed. Going to the throne, he opened the casket, laid it on the couch. Raising his hands he said, 'If these relics shall abide undisturbed by any man soever, and if these relics should endure through all the ages to come and beyond that too, serving as a refuge for the people of this land, then may they rest as the Master lay upon his deathbed, upon this precious couch.'

Indagutta stepped in, together with as many leading monks as could enter. Around the couch they prostrated themselves. Duttha Gamani led Tissa to the entrance. He felt a great weariness and Saliya took his hand as they stood, looking for the last time at the repository and all its wonderful appointments. On the couch lay the form of the Buddha, a dying, deathless Buddha, and around the couch the monks raised their songs of salutation, of grief, of longing. It was the fifteenth day in the bright half of the Asalha month[108] and an *uposatha* day.[109] All over the land, the earth seemed to move as if in a gentle swell and the people broke away, some fearful, although many sensed that this was but a sign from the gods that the ceremonies had their highest approval.

'We will not close the chamber, yet none shall enter. Let the throne of offering be the final reception point of all who come to worship,' Duttha Gamani said.

When the monks emerged, he called for his white parasol of dominion. He stripped himself of all his kingly ornaments, and around him, the people did likewise. Even the dancing girls placed their chains, jewelled anklets and armbands on the curved stone slab. To Saliya he said, 'Go ye and bring up the carts of offerings to the bhikkhus, and let every street be lit with torches, and let torches be fixed on the inner and outer walls and thousands more all over this place that this night be as day. See to it, our son, and have the palace servants attend to it all.'

Indagutta said that the monks would remain on the terraces.

'But first, our offerings, venerable one.'

Carl Muller

'Let them be received in token and taken to the Maha Vihara, for we remain to honour the Blessed One through the night.'

After the offering of garments, sugar, clarified butter and other necessities had been made, the king descended the terraces. It was late, and he was too full of emotion to eat, but he did so on Tissa's urging and was told that his son had gone to the pavilion where Asokamala Devi was, and together with the Naga maidens of her escort, had gone to his palace.

From the upper storey of the palace it was an eerie, but spellbinding sight. The torches made the yellow robes of the monks gleam, and the light, rising and falling, made even their faces a dancing yellow. All over the country, as far as could be seen, the torches flamed, throwing shadows into confusion. The yellow fires seemed to send fingers of gold up the sides of the huge cupola, and overhead, a big moon hung in a cloudless sky, dripping its silver benediction. In the air, the chanting rose and fell. This would go on till the first light of day kissed the rocks of Mihintale.

Duttha Gamani found that sleep would not come. Thinly he heard the salutations of the monks—the *Abhaya Parittha*[110] and the *Ratana Suttanta*.[111] He dozed fitfully. It was the silence that roused him and he saw daylight at his window. Hurriedly he arose, went to the balcony, watched the long line of monks on their way to the Maha Vihara. He caught his breath. The pavilion that stood before the monastery was no more. Surely none but the devas had erected it, and now it was gone. At the baths, he summoned the captain of the guards. 'This be our message—take good note. All the people of this land shall adore the relics throughout this week. The relic chamber will lie open but none shall enter. The monks who will remain at the entrance will receive the offerings that the people bring. See to it that drummers convey this throughout the city and that riders carry it around the land.'

The chief minister came in to announce the thera Indagutta. Receiving the monk after his ablutions, Duttha Gamani agreed with what he had to say: 'It is now for the brotherhood to take the order of the worship of the relics, sire, and of the offerings made. Samaneras will be in constant attendance.'

'Yes, it is good. And there will be many who will bring offerings of great merit, treasures even. All this must we also enshrine.'

'Yes, O King, but in the smaller chamber that lies above. None may tread within the main chamber now.'

With the king's proclamation was added the order of the Sangha that all who would adore the relics arrive together and return early, each to his own home. Over the relic chamber was another smaller repository and a temporary line of steps to it was positioned using compacted earth. Many in the land held, in their personal shrine rooms and in the cetiyas they had constructed, some relics of the Buddha. They were not corporeal relics, but were just as revered. They wished to also deposit these precious items in the Maha Thupa and were pleased that their king gave them leave to do so. 'So far as they are able to do so, the people shall also enshrine such relics as they hold.'

The *Mahavamsa* tells us that the people, 'so far as they could', carried out the enshrining of thousands of relics in the upper chamber.

At length Duttha Gamani said. 'Now let the brotherhood take charge of sealing the chambers, both the lower and the upper. Have we not done all that could be done?'

Indagutta saw the king's anxiety His breathing was

Carl Muller

becoming laboured and there was a sickly cast on his face. He told the samaneras Uttara and Sumana to close the repositories.[112]

Duttha Gamani refused to rest. 'Rest!' he has said in near anger to Tissa. 'What mean you in saying that we must rest? Know you not that the thupa must be completed?'

'At least permit the physicians to look at you, brother. Perhaps they can prescribe an enervating tonic.'

'There!' said the king, pointing to the thupa. 'For years, brother, that has been our tonic. Don't you see that what we started we must complete?'

Tissa was silent...then said, 'What is it we must do? Let me help in every way I can.'

'Yes, we need thy help—and brother, think not that we are angered. Impatience, not anger. We must hasten the task. The chambers must now be further enclosed with side walls of brick. Come. The thupa must be completed.'

On site, Duttha Gamani seemed to be fired with new vigour. The chief of the builders listened and worked with fervour. It was a daunting task, for high up, swarmed the men who would lay the *Caturassacaya*.[113]

'You see, brother,' Tissa said, 'the work presses on. Once the capital is completed, only the spire remains. I will see that the dome is now covered with stucco and while this is being done—and it will be many days—I will return to Ruhuna and see how things fare there. Also, to Dighavapi must I go.'

'But you will return, will you not?'

'That I will, for must I not share in your joy when the thupa is complete?'

Duttha Gamani was troubled. 'We are not happy that you leave, but the south needs your attention too; and yet we are desolate and will have no one to turn to.'

Later, he returned to his chamber, clutching at his chest as he slowly took the steps. He dreaded the nights now, when the cramps came and the nerves of his legs seemed to stand up as thick cords, knotting viciously. Even his bones seemed to hurt and the pillows he laid under his feet gave him scant comfort. Yet it was grudgingly that he asked for the physicians. He could do no more. He asked that his bed be raised, be placed at the open door and that the door remain ever open. From that point he could see the thupa. Yes, the square capital seemed to be complete and the plaster work of the done was slowly beginning to show.

One day, tormented by cramps and with the pain in his chest too much to bear, he cried to his steward, 'Summon the chief minister—and why do these attendants hover about us the way they do? All they do is stand around and stare.' He wanted Tissa. He wanted Saliya.

'But, lord, the prince is not in the city. He has left his mansion.'

'For what reason? And the chandala woman?'

'She has gone too, lord, with the prince. A message has been sent to Dighavapi, where King Tissa now is, that he may come in haste.'

'When—when will he be here?'

'Perhaps in two days, sire.'

Duttha Gamani groaned. 'And what of the physicians? We need to recover. Do not they know that?'

The chief minister paled. Too well he knew that his king was very ill. The physicians had consulted the rishis, and those wise men had shaken their heads gravely. The king's illness was mortal. He was wasting away. 'I—I have said in the message that King Tissa must come at once, lord, and impressed the urgency of his coming.'

'Yes, yes, that you have said already...and the physicians?'

'They are even now in consultation with the rishis. We have men ready to go to the lands beyond if there is anything that must be brought that is necessary to return thee to health, sire.'

Duttha Gamani waved a hand weakly in dismissal. 'Bring our brother to us no sooner he arrives.'

It was sooner than even the chief minister had expected. Tissa had left Dighavapi, riding furiously to the river ford. Somehow he knew that his brother was calling to him. And the dream! Why was his mother leaning over him, urging him to go to Anuradhapura? Was it a dream? He had heard himself saying even in his half-sleep, 'Mother...is it you?' And it was her, standing by his couch with large sad eyes. 'Go, my son. Rise, go at once. Your brother needs you. Help him to rest his mind, be happy, for soon will he set his feet on the road to immortality. Go! Go now!'

He was tearing off the coverlet even as he awoke, raced to plunge into the waters of the Dighavapi tank, dashing the sleep out of him as he mounted his horse. He called to his son, Thulathanaka, to mount up. 'Father—what, what is it?'

'We ride to the north. Bring you a second horse as well. Nothing must bar our progress. Hurry! Your uncle is dying!'

At the Kacchaka ford they met the messengers. 'Yes, we know, and what do the physicians say?'

'We know not, lord, but here is the letter from the chief minister.'

Yes, the king was surely dying. 'You! Give us your horse. It is faster than ours. And take our son's horse too. Saddle the spare pony. Mind you not push the animals. Return to the city at an easy pace. We go with all speed. See that the horses do not fill their bellies with water.'

It was late afternoon, and Tissa took the shaded roads, accepting the cover of the huge trees, knowing that the horses needed it. When they entered the outer walls it was very late and the sounds of their hoof beats echoed in the near-empty street. Thulathanaka stretched himself upright in the saddle. Never had he ridden so hard, so far, before. At the inner gate, they dismounted, called for the stablemen. 'See that there is some salt in the water and the grain that you give to them. And keep wraps on their backs until the sweat dries.'

They entered the palace to be met by a surprised chamberlain. 'The rishis are in the king's chamber, lord, and the Brahmin priests have also been summoned to read the signs.'

'That is not what we wish to hear. What of the king's condition? And why is the palace so ill-lit? Is it that many here are asleep even while their king lies ailing. Go to! Rouse the palace! Let all the lamps be lit. What of the monks? Have they not been told? Come, our son, we will bathe and take food—see that a meal is served in the lower hall—and then will we seek out the physicians.'

The physicians shook their heads. 'There is naught we can do, lord, for the king has himself ignored the signs and warnings of his illness that now eats into him. He rejected our advice even when we wished to tell of this to him. Above all, he even rejected the bodily sustenance that would have given him, even now, some strength to combat this malady. He scarcely rested. He scarcely ate. It amazes us to think of how he drove himself with no thought of his needs. The obsessions of his mind ruled him, sire.'

Tissa could not fault them. Rest? Tonics? How angered

Duttha Gamani had been even when he had suggested these. Wryly he thought: 'Yes, always the disobedient one.'

'Tell us, good sirs, how long can he remain in this state?'

'That is difficult to say. But now the king's rest is enforced and that is a good thing. At least the body has a chance to rest, build itself. But there is no real hope, sire. Even now we cannot say if it will be another week or another three months. It is a strange disease. It consumes him from within and it moves seemingly slowly. It is not how soon the king will die but how soon the disease will bring on his death. The king could even live for many months more.'

'But—but this is monstrous! Each new day in a life such as you describe. Will not there be more pain?'

'Yes, sire.'

'And can you not alleviate such suffering?'

'We have such substances, but that will place him in a state of semi-consciousness…lord, we see the pleading in his eyes. He wishes to keep his eyes, his mind, on the Maha Thupa. Were we to kill the pain, we will kill all sensation. We will also kill his senses. We cannot do so, sire. Were he to die, will not he die, his dream unrealized? What a heavy burden will that be upon us.'

Rushing to the king's chamber, Tissa saw the glad light in his brother's eyes. His voice was clipped. 'No,' he said, 'do not talk. Do not try to move yourself. I have returned and the thupa will be completed. I promise you, my brother, that you will see it in its final glory. Rest now, and make yourself as comfortable as you can. See, your broth is untouched. Will you not take of it now that I have returned?' He called for a steward. 'The king will eat. See that he takes all the broth and more if he wishes.' He told Duttha Gamani, 'At dawn tomorrow, I will be on site, and

I will not return until the thupa is completed. And my son will remain with thee and will summon me if needs me.'

'Your son—who...?'

'Thulathanaka, the youngest. Lanja Tissa, the elder boy, rules the south.'

'We would...we would like...like to see the boy.'

'Of course, and no finer son, I warrant. He will stay by you. He thinks you are the greatest of heroes. He will cheer you up with his chatter.'

'Will you...tell the thera...the thera Indagutta?'

'That I will. Indeed, the brotherhood must be informed. I cannot think why this has not been done.' He touched the king's cheek. 'You are loved full well, brother, and when you are surrounded with love and the prayers of all who love you, will you not know happiness? So many will beseech the gods on your behalf. Rest now. You will know what it is to live in the peace of the greatness you have wrought.'

Tissa felt the tiredness creep over him. He would rest. He would not entrap himself the way his brother had done. What had the physicians said? Obsession! Yes, that grand magnificent obsession—and to what end? A grander, more terrible sacrifice? He banged his fist on the table. 'They should lay my brother within the thupa!' he gritted. Rising he went to his chamber.

In another room Thulathanaka snored. Tissa allowed himself a smile. Doubtless, he would snore too.

He did.

In his chamber, Duttha Gamani's chest puffed and collapsed with the shortness of his breath—but he slept and he dreamed of a ladder that rose to a place he could not see. He had his feet on the lower rungs and as he climbed, he felt no cramp in his legs.

The first steps on the long road to immortality.

PAST LIFE, FUTURE MERIT

It was time to seal—to close up forever the relic chamber.

When we consider the wealth of art—the statues, paintings, the immense scope of the work executed, this reference to Buddhist art brings us to ask whether all this derived from a well-established artisan tradition or whether it found its way into Duttha Gamani's Great Stupa from outside Lanka. Indeed, we have to accept that the seven paintings of scenes representing the seven places where the Buddha spent his first seven weeks after his enlightenment[114] had not been known to exist before, and were first executed on Duttha Gamani's orders. This would confirm the existence of long-established and skilled artisans' guilds. These scenes are found in the image houses of viharas all over Sri Lanka today, giving us 2,400 years of unbroken tradition—the longest-lived depiction of any single body of subject matter in the history of art. The paintings made the relic chamber a true gallery of the most exquisite art of the times. Besides the seven depictions, lovingly done, there were thirty-two other paintings as well as magnificent renditions of the Buddha's previous existences as told of in the Jatakas,[115] the Tusita Heaven, and the Bodhi Tree.

It would be interesting to consider the thirty-two paintings, even briefly, if only to impress on and be impressed by the strong fervour that made of the Lanka of old a truly Buddhist land. There was the 'Entreaty of Brahma' where Brahma asked leave of the Buddha to reveal what he had discovered of the world. The Buddha, it is said, was reluctant, for wisely he knew that such would be too profound to be understood by one and all.

The painting showing the Buddha's first sermon is found today in temples all over the island. Here in the Deer Park—the Isipatana—near Gaya, the Buddha set in motion the Wheel of the Truth. The painting depicted the preaching of the four Noble Truths to the five ascetics who had awaited the Master's coming. For five years, the Buddha had lived with these ascetics until he realized that the extremes of their ascetic path—the aramana—would not bring enlightenment. With his return and his doctrine of the Middle Way, the ascetics rejected their lives of deprivation and became the Buddha's first disciples. There was also 'The Disciplining of the Jatilas' showing the conversion of three ascetics named Gaya, Nadi and Uruvela Kassapa. Again, there was 'The Eighty Disciples'—the conversion of that many, following the conversion of Sariputta and Mogallana.[116] This theme, too, is usually found in many of today's image houses, taking up an entire wall. What is interesting to know is that many of these disciples, as depicted, have identical images as they are drawn on either side of the Buddha. This has been done with the use of leather templates to paint in the most prominent features as with the use of stencils. The templates are turned over to reverse the orientation when drawing the figures that stand in the opposite direction.[117]

'The Journey to Kapilavattu' depicted the miracle of the

Carl Muller

gems—the gem-strewn promenade—where the Buddha, on his way to preach to the Sakyas, the members of his own family clan, cast gems into the air so that, when they fell, they formed a path upon which he trod.

There was also 'The Ordination of Rahula and Ananda'. Rahula, the Buddha's son, and Ananda, the stepbrother, became great and pious monks. In 'The Sermon in the Tavatimsa Heaven' it is said, the Buddha ascended to preach to his own mother who resided there. The sermon was the *Abidhamma*, the Third Basket of Wisdom. He then returned from this celestial abode of the thirty-three gods.

'The Assembly of the Questioning of the Thera' depicted how the Buddha demonstrated the wisdom of his disciple Sariputta before an assembly at the gates of Sankapura. 'The Advice to Rahula' showed the preaching of the *Rahulovadasuttas* at Veluvana near Rajagaha, and again at Jetavana. 'The Assembly of Dhanapala' was of a different aspect altogether, for it showed the malice and jealousy of the Buddha's own cousin Devadatta. This painting showed an angry elephant, set loose by Devadatta to crush the Buddha. Many sources give this elephant different names. The Buddha's gentle manner stopped the raging beast in its tracks.

A favourite to this day in many temples is 'The Disciplining of Alavaka, Angulimala and Apalala'. In the main, artists today concentrate on Angulimala who was an arch-criminal in the times of the Buddha and whose practice it was to chop off the thumbs of all he killed and string them to wear as a necklace. In many country viharas in Sri Lanka today, we find local artists taking special delight in painting the thumbs gushing blood that gives to the demon-faced Angulimala a bloody, hideous character. Usually the hair is also made to stand on end and the eyeballs protrude. Angulimala's goal was to wear one thousand thumbs around his neck, but when he had strung together 999, he is said to have lost his chain and had to begin all over again. Seeing the Buddha on a village road, he approached, intent on murder, but found himself stalking an impossible victim. However slowly the Buddha walked, Angulimala could not overtake him, however swiftly he ran. Finally, the Buddha stopped, turned around and preached to him, and he was converted. There is also the painting, 'The Assembly of the Parayanas'—another conversion of a Brahman tribe of Rajagaha.

'The Relinquishing of the Span of Life' showed the Buddha amid a heaving Earth. This earthquake is believed to have occurred when the Buddha decided to give up further living at the end of three months. Obviously, the paintings in progression on the walls of the relic chamber were now nearing the end time of the Buddha's earthly career. The next showed 'The Acceptance of the Sukkaramaddava and the Pair of Gold Garments'. There was particular pathos in this depiction, for it showed how even the hapless ironmonger, Cuda, could have unwittingly brought upon the world, the 'end time' . The *sukkaramaddava* is the dish of tainted food[118] which Cuda gave to the Buddha. Eating this, the Buddha took fatally ill. Even as death approached, a pair of exquisite gold garments were offered him by Malla Pukussa, and it is told how the disciple Ananda dressed the Master in them. And yet, the Buddha's body glowed with a brightness even greater than that of the garments—a certain sign that death was near. Ananda then wished to give to his Master a last drink of water and, as the next painting showed, the disciple needed to perform a miracle too. In 'The Drinking of Clear Water' was depicted the wondrous cleansing of the dirty waters

Carl Muller

of the Kalukuttha River, so that Ananda could bring to his dying Master a last drink of clear water.

'The Worshipping of the Feet by the Thera' showed the thera Mahakassapa bowed at the dead Buddha's feet. It is said that when the grieving assembly of monks tried to ignite the Buddha's pyre, it would not light, and it could not be set alight until Mahakassapa arrived from Pava to adore his Master's feet. It was only then, and after Mahakassapa had circumambulated the pyre three times, and uncovered the Buddha's feet, that the pyre caught fire, igniting by itself.

The next two paintings showed 'The Quenching of the Fire'—the streams of rain sent upon the pyre by the devas so that the corporeal relics of the Buddha may be retrieved; and 'The Distribution of the Relics by Dona'—the squabble over the relics until the Brahmin Dona divided them into eight equal portions. A fitting final painting indeed, for the chamber was to hold one of these eight portions, or donas.

Naturally, archaeologists today who would accept the fabulous ornamentation and decoration of the main repository, would also accept that it was in proportion to the size of the cupola: a most extensive chamber. It had to be, obviously, for it held many other costly fittings too. And who would not doubt that, for a king, for a people of 76 BC this was a stupendous achievement indeed!

And now, it was time to enclose these treasures, mask them from the gleaming white of the stucco, cover the fat-coloured entrance stones, that to the one who raises his eyes there would be not a trace of the glory within.

Tissa knew that, even with the best will in the world, the dagaba would never be completed. He had talked to the builders and, fearful of great heights as he was, had stood upon the tee, his knees trembling, wondering at the swaying land below. He was white-faced and perspiring even as he learned how impossible it would be to do all that yet remained to be done.

When he had to descend to the terraces far below, he accepted the suggestion that he be lowered in a strong chair and with the aid of three stout ropes...and he would have the chair face the stupa so that he would not have to look upon the land as he was slipped slowly to the ground. Why was his mouth so full of salt? When he stumbled away, he spat and spat again and felt his stomach heave. It was only when he had reached the spot where the trenches had been cut for the parapet wall that he felt he was safe and on firm ground again.

What was he to do? Would not his brother heap death's last reproach on him? Moodily he walked away, climbed the hill with it's spreading trees of *Madu*,[119] *Ehela*[120] and *Tammanu*[121] and found himself on the bund of the Tissa Wewa. The morning was clear and the waters lapped the rocks with sucking sounds. What could he do? Could he make Duttha Gamani understand, accept, that it was all so impossible? And rashly had he promised! The builders had said four months. Four months! With a deep sigh, almost a groan, he squatted between the slabs of rock that fringed the water's edge. His mother would have been able to talk the king into acceptance of what had so far been done as enough for a lifetime, but he had not the will to be as persuasive. The breeze seemed to strengthen, break into a sonorous song. Such a slow sort of song, he thought idly. Why, any child could put words to such a plaintive music! *Dying...lying...deceive...believe...*suddenly his head jerked up. It was a song, and he knew that voice. His

Carl Muller

mother was singing somewhere around him. He turned his head, trying to catch the words, the message of those soft words, each ending with a rustling sigh...*Deception done to ease the dying...with love deceive that love believe...*

Tissa rose, looked up, then at the water with its patterns of sunlight that seemed to spread like speckled gold. Yes, surely it was his mother. It was the same sad voice of his Dighavapi dream... *A love that lies deludes the eyes...* He wanted to cry out to her, but the voice held him silent... *Illusion causes death's delusion...A dream to weave that life may leave...*

'Illusion!' Tissa exclaimed. 'Is this what I must now do?' And again the words: *With love deceive that love believe...with love delude that death intrude...* and the wind stilled and the sun blazed down and he ran down the bank, knowing what he must do.

He rushed to the Maha Vihara, told the thera Indagutta in a breathless voice: 'Occupy my brother, good sir; take his mind away, his eyes away from the Maha Thupa. I must have opportunity to complete it even if what I do is just pretence.'

The thera looked at Tissa with sadness and sympathy. 'Is it that you will show your brother what is not there?'

'Aye. It is the only way. I have stood upon the caturassacaya. I have talked to the builders. Four months, they say. Tell me, venerable sir, is the king to die without seeing the thupa complete?'

'I can occupy him, yes...he shall lie in the great hall and will meet all the holy theras of the land, and also, we can call for the reading of the Book of Meritorious Deeds.'

'Yes, yes, but he must remain in the hall for many days.'

'Twelve days...will that be sufficient for your purpose?'

'Longer if it is possible. Surely the audience with the brotherhood can be prolonged...'

'Yes, it can be. We can tell of many things, fill his mind with the past. Yes, we will make time that you present your artifice. But, O King, how will it be done?'

Tissa told him.

Duttha Gamani had no wish to be moved but could not refuse the Maha Thera. 'Lord king, from every point in the island have the brethren come, hearing of thy illness. Who could accommodate such a number in thy bedchamber? Thus has the great hall been prepared and a couch upon which you may recline, and beside you will remain the son of your brother who wishes to be with thee at all times.'

Duttha Gamani smiled faintly. 'Yes, a boy who is as our true son. It was our brother's happy thought indeed, to bring him to us. But the Maha Thupa...'

'Have you not charged your brother with its completion? That will he do. Know you, O King, that in today's early hours he stood upon the capital, directing the foundation of the spire.'

'What? Up there? Why, our brother dislikes heights. Ever since he sat upon our elephant and was unseated, he has this fear of high places.'

'He will complete the thupa. And you cannot ignore the brethren who come here to comfort thee.'

'Then we will move as you say, good sir...Yet...'

Indagutta did not stay to listen. Soon, strong servants came in and with care, the king was carried to the great hall where a splendid place had been prepared with silken curtains to be drawn that the king may sleep; and the tables laden with offerings he could make as he wished to all who came; and attendants at the pillars, against each pillar being placed small curved-legged tables holding everything from cosmetics to oils and unctions, goblets of fresh water, cloaks and wraps. Even the barber, the master of the bedchamber, the messengers, the girls who would sing softly as the king reposed, the slaves to carry away the spittoons, and the servers of fruit and sweetmeats had gathered and there would they remain, they were told, until they were no longer needed.

Duttha Gamani looked with tired eyes upon the monks.[122] Even as his eyes fell on each group, they sang their chorus of prayer for his health and well-being. He reached for Thulathanaka's arm. 'We are pained,' he said, 'for among all these holy ones we see not Theraputtabhaya.'

'Is it your champion that you speak of, Uncle?'

'It is, it is. So mighty a warrior was he. Throughout our campaign, even as we marched hither, twenty-eight battles did we fight and with his mighty club, never did he yield his ground.' Suddenly there came a new light in his eyes. 'Ah, such days were those.'

'My uncle, the songs of your heroic campaign are still sung ceaselessly in the south.'

A look of pain crossed the king's face. 'But why is he not here? He asked our leave to take the robes, retired to the pious life on the Panjali Mountain beside the Kirinda.[123] Is it that he knows that our death struggle has begun and that we lose this last battle?'

Thera Indagutta shot a worried look. If the king grew distressed he may well wish to return to his chamber. With a powerful surge of mental energy, he bid Theraputtabhaya to show himself. *Stand ye before your king. Be ye his champion as in the past!*

Far south, Theraputtabhaya called to the monks of the temple. 'You who have overcome the cravings rise with me. We go to stand before our king!'

Like a cloud-arrow, they pierced the air, a saffron column of 500, and the trees bowed their branches as they descended. Duttha Gamani's face lit up. 'Ah, but we are mistaken, nephew. He is here. Go bid him approach.'

The robed warrior sat before his king, recited the verse that the god Sakka said after the death of the Buddha:

Anicca vata samkhara uppadavayadhammino
Uppajjitva nirujjhanti tesam vupasamo sukkho

(Transcient are, alas! the samkharas, having the nature of growth and decay; Having been produced, they are dissolved again; blissful is their subjection.)

Duttha Gamani said in a light voice: 'That we do not fully understand, brave one, but we are glad, nay, heartened beyond measure, to see thee. Formerly did we not fight—the ten great warriors by our side? But now we fear we have entered a battle with death, and this foe... how can we conquer?'

'O King, but why dost thou fear? This foe that is death is unconquerable unless the foe that is sin is conquered. All that has come into this fleeting existence, this transitory existence, must necessarily perish. The perishable is all that exists. That is what I recited, and this is what the Master taught. Death comes even to the Buddhas who are untouched by shame and fear. Therefore, think you: all that is must perish and full of sorrow, the real becomes unreal. Know you not of your last mortal existence, O King? Listen then, for I will tell thee, even as this day ends and another yet awaits thee.'

The time of the noonday meal was long past, and it was late when the monks were offered soft foods and naught else. It was mellowing, and the day had cooled

Carl Muller

when Thcraputtabhaya said: 'This is thy story, O King, and thy love for the true doctrine has ever been great. Even then was the world of gods within thy grasp, yet did you turn away from the celestial to return to the womb of the queen, to fulfil her destiny and thine.[124] And how much glory have you brought to the doctrine even as you declared sole sovereignty. Is it not through your will, your steadfastness, even when called the disobedient one, that you made this one land under one umbrella and with one true faith. Think, O King, of the merits of thy existence then and now. Thou art rich, nay, overflowing with merit. Death is not thy foe. It will come to thee with love and a promise of comfort and greater joy.'

Indagutta came up. 'And now rest ye, O King, for tomorrow will we assemble to tell you more. The evening closes and your nights will be peaceful and untroubled.'

'Yes. Have we not our champion now? Even in our single combat ahead will he be beside us.'

That night, in the great hall, Duttha Gamani slept peacefully, and soundly too. Even the servants around his bed remarked that he scarcely stirred and the harsh sound of his breathing was barely heard.

Twelve days...It took all of twelve days, and all the while Duttha Gamani lay in the great hall. Twelve days for Tissa was barely enough.

'What does our brother do and how fares he?' he asked the thera Indagutta on the sixth day.

'We now read to him of his merits. So much has he performed that is worthy. It may be many days yet.'

Tissa was pleased. 'And is he well?'

'He seems strengthened. There is an air of confidence, but the physicians say we must not be deceived. The end draws closer.'

'Yes. We must hurry.'

Brothers...kings...one worked in a frenzy, the other slipped gently towards that long sleep...one driven to exhaustion to keep his word...the other at rest, waiting with that faraway look in his eyes for the promise to be kept...in both of them the face of great love and an unshakeable faith.

The *Punnapotthaka* is the Register of Deeds of Piety and Merit. The scribe brought it into the great hall, and it was given to the scribe to read from it. It contained a faithful record of the works of the king, contained on many pages. The book was brought on Indagutta's bidding, for he wished that the hours be filled with a recitation of the king's meritorious deeds and that time be also taken to recapitulate. In this way would time be bought, enabling Tissa to complete his work.

The record was impressive indeed. Ninety-nine viharas had Duttha Gamani built and nineteen kotis of cash had he spent on the Maricavati Vihara.[125]

'May we remind, O King, that this vihara remains a treasure that gives to the kingdom the five advantages,' Indagutta said. 'Again, this has come through the special wisdom of thy pious and selfless deeds. Treasures there are, built or stored by the vain and impious, but they carry the blot of the five faults.'

'Tell us what these five are—both good and bad.'

'The treasures of the wise and good are possessed by

the land that is well-governed, O King, as this land is. It enjoys popularity among all men and the high esteem of the pious. It also enjoys fame. Always is there fidelity in the fulfilment of duty, and to its ruler Heaven awaits after death.'

'And no blot of fault is there?'

'No, sire. Such faults will bring about loss by fire, water, the depredations of men and animals, the seizure and confiscation of land by enemies and the raids of enemies even unto war. None of these has arisen to trouble thy reign.'

The scribe read on. 'Thirty kotis did the king expend on the splendid Lohapasada...' and again Indagutta reminded the king of this gleaming monastery and how he had wished that no work on it be done without amply rewarding the workers. Yes, there was much to be said, much to spin out the hours. The canny thera even invited the king to tell of what came to his mind, and in this way did the days pass and each day saw the king fortified by the enumeration of all the good of his life.

'It is like a medicine, I believe,' said Thulathanaka in a low voice. 'See, he sleeps. I will go to my father, reassure him.'

ILLUSION AND DELUSION

EVEN TISSA COULD NOT RIGHTLY SAY HOW MANY BOLTS OF WHITE cotton cloth had been used. It had been shrewdly decided that existing feudal service systems be brought into play in order that the huge work be speedily executed. To this end were the *Nilakarayas*[126] pressed into service, and, for the purposes of Tissa's massive deception, the *Hannawli*.[127] The feudal system of the state had its like system in the feudal caste service organization of the vihara and the devale, and it was necessary for the maha theras to commission the tenants of the temple lands to perform the work, since Tissa was not king of the whole island.

The work was done with a furious sense of urgency. The cloth had to be brought even by riverboats from the north-west, by fast horse carts from the south, by men who poled their rafts from the north-east. It was a simple enough expediency, but Tissa had to make certain that nothing of what he planned would reach his brother's ears. He was as a man possessed, and one day, with scarce heed for his own dignity, he had stormed at the chamberlain: 'We do not care that the king grows overtired in the great hall! Nor do we care that he ails and how restless he is! Occupy his every waking moment. Let him not know of what we do at the Maha Thupa!'

Finally, with the cloth ready, he summoned the *Kinniyas*.[128] He had already given an outline of his needs to the monks who had to ensure that everything would be attended to. The weavers would plait a mock spire which would be mounted on the tee, and that would not be all: the reed spire would then be covered, painted cunningly with lacquer and *Kankutthaka*.[129] In addition to the plaiters, parasol-frame weavers were also pressed into service. They were needed to assemble a mock parapet that would encircle the pinnacle. Also, the *Sittereo*[130] and the *Tarahallo*[131] were commissioned to make the necessary ornamentation.

Had Duttha Gamani stood on his balcony he would have surely seen what was, from a distance, a miracle of sorts. On the tee stood the chiefs of the tailors, ready to drop the long trains of cloth. The trestles had been moved away from the massive cupola in order that the cloth fell true and unhindered. When all was ready, the cloths were released, falling like long white cloud cascades, falling in broad flowing sheets, falling to the very base and piling upon the terraces, where seamstresses cut the lengths to size. In the sunshine, the dagaba blazed white fire and Tissa waited for the monks to tell him that the cloths had fallen true.

'Every part is covered, lord. The frames can be moved back that the painters begin.'

'Move back the trestles then, but let the painters do their work on the spire first, then descend to complete their tasks.'

It was no easy task. On the parapet of the pinnacle it was necessary to paint the sun and moon motifs, while the picture of the sun on the four sides of the tee also needed to be done. The goldsmiths made the drawings and the cleverly indented lines that would give to each emblem a mounded appearance. The artists were then lowered to the base and the terraces to complete their work, while beating up and along the trestles, the tailors secured each length of cloth, ensuring that a smooth look would present itself, unruffled by wind—enough to make a dying man believe that dreams do come true.

On the cloth were painted railings, a panelled basement, representtations of filled vases and ornaments that radiated like the five fingers.[132]

In the great hall there was little doubt that Duttha Gamani was growing weaker. 'One more day,' pleaded Thulathanaka. 'My father asks for but one more day. Give him of your strength, Theraputtabhaya, for he thinks of your might and grows strong.'

The warrior monk clapped his hands. 'I will read to the king of his merits. This scribe is a dreary reader.' He took the Book of Merit and struck his chest. 'O King, remember ye the two precious earrings you gave to the mountain people of Kotta in the time of the Akkhakhayika famine? Truly is the record of thy merits abundant. Will you not tell us—tell all who have gathered here in love of what you have done, great one?'

Duttha Gamani waved a protesting hand. 'Is it that we must tell of our deeds? There are many, and they will surely make tiresome listening.'

'But is that not what a king of great valour and pride must do? Listen, O monks, and tell me if you can say why the people of the mountain called it the Akkhakhayika famine. Who will tell us? What, have you then lost the wit of words?'

'We hear it to have been the Pasanachataka famine,' said a monk, 'and yet you call it by the name of the seeds that the peasants use in the throwing of dice in their village games.'

'Because it is true and wholly appropriate, O monks. Know you that so great was the hunger of the time that the people of Kotta had to eat the nuts of the Akkha.[133] Who cared to toss the dice when hungry? This was the great famine and it was our lord's gift that brought for the people sour millet and the grain they hungered for. Such merit has our king earned, venerable ones. Why, who will think back to the days when the father of the young prince among us wished to battle his own brother, our king? The noble Thulathana, who leaves not the side of our monarch, may know of this. The blood of a victor flows in his veins too, does it not? Yes, my prince, think not less of thy father even as you think much of your uncle, for even our great lord will own that he was vanquished by thy father in the battle of Culanganiya.'

'That do I know,' said Thulathanaka, 'but...'

Duttha Gamani smiled. 'There are no buts, dear nephew. Love your father as we love him, for we were both headstrong in our youth. Know you not that it is to us that was given the name Duttha? Ambition can be a blinding thing, nephew. We turn our eyes away from ourselves and see not the wrong we do.'

'It is the true greatness of one who admits to his frailties,' said Theraputtabhaya, 'but listen, for I will tell you more. Even as our king fled the forces of his brother, then rested to take a midday meal, did the ascetic Tissa come to him...and did not the king give to him the food from his own bowl? That is the stamp of greatness, O monks, for whether in victory or in defeat, the brotherhood was first in our king's mind and heart.'

Duttha Gamani listened, then raised a hand. 'Truly do you say too much. Let us instead tell it in a manner as simple as we can. Listen, venerable ones, for we need no book to tell us of what we have done. And yet do we say, all has been done for the glory of the doctrine. This is why we are your king. We have given great and costly alms to all of the land and have held twenty-four great Vesakha festivals,[134] and on three occasions have we bestowed garments for the brotherhood of all this land. Five times, and each time for seven days, have we bestowed with glad and willing heart, the rank of ruler of this land upon the doctrine, and this have we made manifest with the lighting of a thousand lamps. In every place where the sick be, have we bestowed nourishment and remedies and also rice foods with honey and oil and great *jala* cakes [135] baked in butter and also quantities of rice…and…and have we not marked the uposatha festivals with the distribution of lamps to the eight great viharas of the land…' Theraputtabhaya noticed how the king's breath became laboured. 'Allow me to tell of thy great endeavours, O King. I beg leave to do so.'

Duttha Gamani raised a hand, then let it fall weakly.

'Know you all who have assembled here that our lord, who wished that the doctrine be spread, even wished to preach the suttas of the Buddha himself. Ah, but that was not pride, good sirs. Only a desire to set in motion what he most wished for. Such a day was that, I recall. And is it not true that the gift of preaching the doctrine is more than the giving of worldly riches? There, at the foot of the Lohapasada was the preacher's chair, and there, said our king, would he preach the *Mangala Sutta* to the

Carl Muller

brotherhood.[136] Was it that our lord presumed much? Nay, O monks, for even if he were a preacher of distinction, and even if he did sit in the preacher's chair, and even though he knew the victory sermon of the Buddha full well, not a word could he say. Humility sat upon him, good monks. The true humility of one who knew he could not set himself over the Order. He rose, and asked instead to listen. And he asked that the preachers carry the message of the Master throughout the land, and much did he give to all who carried forth the doctrine. Here...his gifts to the preachers are written: a *nali*[137] of butter, molasses and sugar as well as sticks of liquorice, four inches long...also did he give the preachers a pair of garments each. And see how well he knew the gladness within him. What causes him to rejoice even now? Ah, it is not of what we know he has so far given but of what he has given heedless of his own life and safety. In times of his greatest adversity has he given, and surely this counts for much.' He paused, knowing that everyone hung on his words. Even Duttha Gamani looked at him keenly.

'It was the time of the famine, O King. When thy earrings were sold and the sour millet and grain obtained for those that starved, did you not offer alms of the sour millet, thy own share, to the five theras that appeared? You would go hungry, but that did not count. The people thanked you. The people ate, but you could not eat with them. Such alms, freely given, wrought much, O King. Know you that of the five theras was Malayamahadeva...so worthy of thy sacrifice. Know you all that this sainted thera gave of the king's offering—a fifth part of it—miraculously making of it enough and more, to nine hundred bhikkhus on the Sumanakuta Mountain.[138] And the thera Dhammagutta of great power—for it is known that with but a single thought he can make the Earth shake—this great thera increased his fifth share of the alms that he could carry it to the five hunded bhikkhus of the Kalyanika Vihara.[139] And such was the power of thy sacrificial gift, O King, that the thera Dhammadinna increased his share in order to feed 12,000 bhikkhus in Piyangudipa.'[140]

Duttha Gamani raised himself slightly. 'All this from a single bowl of gruel...where did this thera Dhammadinna live?'

'In Talanga, sire.'[141]

'And each of these five theras who came to us distributed their bowls of gruel throughout the land...this that you say gladdens us beyond measure.'

'Yes, lord. The thera Khudatissa of Mangana[142] took his share, increased miraculously, that 60,000 bhikkhus could eat of it in the Kesala Vihara,[143] and the thera Mahavyaggha gave of his share—and how small is a share of a fifth of a bowl of gruel, O King—to 700 bhikkhus in the Ukkana Vihara. So great was the worth of thy offering, O King.'

Duttha Gamani lay back and his face was calm, his breathing smooth. Theraputtabhaya laid aside the book, went to him. 'Do you rest, great one. Is it that the brotherhood should retire?'

'Our champion...always our champion...' Duttha Gamani's voice was a strained whisper. 'Twenty-four years have we served the brotherhood, been as a patron of the brotherhood. Now our time is short...very short, holy one. Why has not our brother come? And what of the Maha Thupa...but let it be known that even this body will serve as a patron of the brotherhood—there, in the malaka[144] whence the Maha Thupa may be seen, must our body be burnt, so that to the last we remain servant of the Sangha.'

Carl Muller

Theraputtabhaya did not wish his king to think of death. He was about to frame a consoling reply when he heard the sound of the guards moving outside the door. 'Ah,' he said, 'thy brother comes, sire, and see, see, surely he brings thee glad news.'

Tissa strode in, leaned over the royal couch. 'Brother, be glad. That which was yet to be done is now completed.' He saw the warm fire in the king's eyes.

'You mean it, brother...you have done it all? Oh, such a miracle is this! Can we...can we...'

'Brother, it grows dark. Tomorrow...'

'Yes, yes, at dawn!'

'If it be so, but now you must sleep.'

'But now to our chamber must we go. Now. Let the bearers come, and this bed must they place at the door.'

Tissa shot the thera a look, and Theraputtabhaya nodded. 'It will be as you wish, O king. And now, before this assembly will I tell the good news that they all may gather at the thupa tomorrow.'

'Yes, yes...oh, my heart leaps within me. Let the scribe put away the *Punnapothaka*. No more will there be need of it. Truly happy will I die, and truly happy will my spirit lie among these treasures of the faith.'

They carried him to his chamber while he kept turning, peering through the windows, until, when he had taken his position beside the door, he settled himself carefully. There, in the gloom, he saw an immense whiteness, and that was all. His tired eyes could not make out the spire, but the mass of white thrilled his every fibre. 'Finished,' he murmured, 'finished...and we have lived to see it in its true splendour...how white it is...how...how perfect. May our brother merit the favour of the devas—finished...why did we doubt, yes—we thought our brother would not be able to… what thoughts were those…'

His eyes tried to pierce the gathering darkness and the torchlight in his room danced and seemed to devour his sight. Sighing, he dropped his eyelids. So tired. How can anyone feel so tired…An attendant stole in, looked at the sleeping man, then sat at the door. Soon others would come. They would listen to the king's breathing. They would settle his pillows should he toss about and would see that the smoke of the sacred basil wafted lightly and that no insects would trouble him. It was not good that he had refused to keep the chamber door closed. The night brought its vapours too, and no lanterns could be lit. Only the scone torches, for the lanterns attracted mosquitoes. Softly, one played a reed pipe.

Duttha Gamani slept, and on his face was a look of deep peace.

The *Mahavamsa* tells us:

> …lying on a palanquin, the king went thither, and when on his palanquin he had passed round the cetiya, going toward the left, he paid homage to it at the south entrance, and he then, lying on his right side on the couch spread upon the ground, beheld the splendid great thupa, and lying on his left side, the splendid Lohapasada, he became glad at heart, surrounded by the brotherhood of bhikkhus.

The Chronicle also tells us that in all, there were 96 koti bhikkhus who, group by group, recited in chorus. It was, some may say, a cruel deception, but Duttha Gamani was dying. His eyes did not see that the cupola was wrapped in cloth; his dimming eyes did not discern the artifice of the spire. All he saw, soaring to the sky, was his greatest accomplishment, and he had lived to see it in its blinding splendour.

Tissa stayed beside him, faintly anxious. At one point the cloth had creased in its affixing and a lungful of air seemed to have stolen in to push at the wrapping. But his brother's weak eyes saw none of this. The image impinged on Duttha Gamani's mind as a whole—and this wholeness was a proud, eternal symbol of faith. Immortality towered over a dying king, and he felt, as he was carried back, that his mother walked beside him.

In the great hall, he gripped Tissa's hand. 'It is you, brother, who will soon be anointed...you who must complete all the rest...all that must be built for adornment ...the encircling wall among others. This must you do, our brother, and care duly for all. Each evening and morning must flowers be offered and let there be a solemn ob—oblation at the Maha Thupa...yes, morning, noon and before dusk. Let not anything—anything we have instituted in the glory of the doctrine—be neglected or fall into disuse...let...let the brethren comfort us now...we desire to...to listen to the words of the great sage. No, no... move us not. This—this couch—now our bed of death...' Indagutta led the monks in sonorous chant and all over the palace the women covered their heads and faces and prostrated themselves. The words of the Buddha filled the hall and in the temples, the monasteries, the bells began to count the minutes.

Tissa put an arm around his son. 'Go, see that the flags of mourning are raised, that the city halts all activity. Let every house light a lamp and drape the gateposts in white and lay jasmines in the water troughs. No carts must be seen on the roads and none will adorn themselves. Let the incense burners be filled in every home. Send no drummers or horses, our son. Only men to carry the news. The temples will ring the tidings, one to another, that all the land will know.'

Duttha Gamani stared at the vaulted roof with fevered eyes. He murmured to himself, and Tissa knelt at his head. 'Our brother, what is it?'

Duttha Gamani did not hear him. 'But our mother,' he whispered, 'why come you with these gods? Can't they wait until I have heard the words of the Master...do we not know how beautiful the celestial worlds are...yes...we see the chariots...How did these golden carts enter...'

Tissa was alarmed. 'The king's mind wanders,' he said softly. 'Do thou prolong the chant.'

'Yes...yes, our mother knew...these great gods...can they not cease their entreaties for as long as the monks tell of the doctrine...heavens and heavens...is this or that heaven to be—to be my choice...' Suddenly he jerked up a hand. The monks ceased their chanting and the king's look was fearful to behold. 'Our brother,' he called with deep pain in his voice, 'why...why have the monks fallen silent. Do they not wish to go on?'

'But did you not sign them to stop?'

'No, no, no...It is to these gods that we raised our hand. Do you not see them...their celestial carts...and our mother with them...'

Tissa's voice shook. 'How many gods, brother?'

'Do you not see them? Six...in six chariots...from the six heavens...they...they each call to us to go...to go with them...'

'Let the chorus go on,' Tissa said, and told Indagutta, 'He is delirious. He sees things that circle over his head. Ask Theraputtabhaya to draw close, give him strength.'

The warrior monk placed his head close to the king's. 'Is it that you allow fancies to possess thee, even as we seek to give thee peace? How can six chariots with the gods of the six heavens float beneath this roof?'

'Ah, my champion...do you doubt too...yes, we see the grief in our brother's eyes. But...but we do not rave, and... and these we see are not...are not the spectres of death... Do we crave heavenly destiny...see you not the chariots?'

'No, lord.'

'Will you ask that six garlands be tossed up...tossed up over our couch?'

Theraputtabhaya nodded. 'But they will only fall upon thee, O King...Yet, will it be done.'

The chanting stopped in some confusion and every head was raised. There, floating over the king's head were the six garlands. 'See...see...do you not see even now... the garlands hang from each of the chariots. No...no... we are not delirious...and there is no...no madness that grips us in death. See, see...our eyes are clear and our mother beckons. Tell me...what is the best...the best of the heavens?'

The hum of the wondering voices lay as an underdamper of sound over which the king's voice was clear and strong.

'Sire,' said Theraputtabhaya, 'happy be the one who rises to the Tusita heaven, for there dwells the Buddha who is to come.'

'Yes—the Tusita heaven. There do we choose to go...and our mother...with...us...' The voice, so strong for those fleeting moments, seemed to break within itself and the last word was a sibilant whisper.

Tissa touched his brother's face, then the sides of the neck. The eyes stared at him and he was startled to see a strange light in them. When he made to draw a hand over the lids, he checked, gasped. In his brother's dead eyes he saw the shining face of his mother.

'Close his eyes swiftly,' Theraputtabhaya said, and put out his own hand to draw down the lids.

Duttha Gamani, lion of Lanka, was dead.

The *Saddharmlamkaraya* tells us that Duttha Gamani was reborn spontaneously as a god in the chariot that carried him to the Tusita heaven; and that he descended from the chariot, clad in resplendent garments, floated to the Maha Thupa which he cicled thrice. Then, after worshipping the community of monks, he was led away to his heavenly abode, rising in the air, surrounded by thousands of celestial beings; and it was his mother who led him to his heavenly reward.

Who could really know?

For Tissa, who would sit the Lion Throne as Saddha Tissa, was the task of the cremation, the rites and rituals. Then would the cloths be torn away, the mock spire removed. The Maha Thupa had to be completed, and he wondered: 'Even among the celestials, as a celestial himself, did not my brother know of my deceit?'

But his brother was dead. It did not matter any more whether the illusion, the delusion, had been right or wrong. Yet Tissa could not help feeling that he had cheated time, cheated his brother, cheated even the gods.

He shook his head, went in to send directions to his son in Ruhuna.

Carl Muller

PEACE...AND THE END
OF PEACE

KING SADDHA TISSA WAS WORRIED. GLADLY HAD HE ACCEPTED kingship, and the land, after the first waves of mourning, after the shockwaves of Duttha Gamani's death, remained in a state of peace. He could not refuse the Lion Throne of Anuradhapura although he could not help thinking somewhat wryly of Saliya...and where was this strange nephew of his? It annoyed him to think of the irresponsibility of the prince who had forsaken both kingdom and princedom. It annoyed him to think of the south, too, for he had this deep sense of unease. His eldest son, Lanja Tissa,[145] now ruled the south and he was too... too cock-a-hoop, if this modern word is the best that could be used. Yes, Lanja Tissa was too full of himself. A good ruler, but there was too much ambition in the youth's eyes and somehow, Saddha Tissa felt, a cruel cast of the mouth. He sighed, then shrugged. It was surely the curse upon the race, he thought: rivalry, enmity, even among the best of siblings. Had he not set himself against his own brother as well? Yes, peace...but for how long?

He had told his younger son: 'Do you remain here, for

your brother spreads his dominion over the south in our name. It is wise that you stay here, by our side.'

Thulathanaka longed for the easier, fiercer, more challenging life of the south. Also he missed the wild coasts and the waves that thundered upon the rocks at night, and the wind that whistled like a hundred sharp knives upon the grindstones of the cliffs. But something in his father's voice stifled his protest. All he said was, 'But it is a large region, and surely my brother needs help.'

'Perhaps he does,' said Saddha Tissa, 'but do we not need your help too? Do you not know that there is much to be done?'

Thulathanaka knew that his father did not really need him. Anuradhapura had the finest builders and craftsmen. The guilds of the artisans were active and well represented. In coming here, he had marvelled at the layout of the city. Much had he learnt about it for, even in Ruhuna, there were many who would tell of the city and its glorious story. He had wandered around it—the road to the resting place of the arahats, the garden of the Sangha, the upper ferry of the Malwatta River. He had even remarked: 'But there is a difference, is there not, father? I see a sacred city and also a city. Did not the saintly Mahinda give to this city the boundaries of the sacred precincts?'

Saddha Tissa had frowned. 'It is hard to say, our son. Now many say, and the Sangha claims it too, that the political city is also the sacred city...but yes, the venerable Mahinda did fix the boundaries of sacred ground. Oh, what does it matter? Your uncle declared the whole land as sacred. Many are the times when faith is fuelled by ignorance, and who can tell what is the wisest course?'

Thulathanaka was restless. He felt that his father had his own reasons for keeping him in Anuradhapura. True, he had had occasion to clash with his brother time and again. He could not forget how Lanja Tissa had always slighted the youngest, Khallata Naga, who was still a boy and looked upon as one of little consequence. Lanja Tissa was a fierce-tempered man with a bad mouth that betrayed ambition and yes, avarice. But they had known their places under the king, their father. Why did his father wish to keep him here?

Saddha Tissa had done much. He completed the spire of the Maha Thupa and had the whole edifice plastered and painted. The spire was crowned with a golden pinnacle and the wall around the *Salapatala Maluwa*[146] raised and adorned with four hundred elephant faces. This elephant wall,[147] with the impression of the foreparts of the elephant jutting forward, was most effective. As Harischandra[148] has said, the elephants all around seemed to be watching the thupa. Saddha Tissa was weary. It was the rudest of shocks to rise one night, see the fierce glow in the sky and rush out to see a great pillar of fire rising above the trees. Screams and shouts tattered the air and he flung aside his wraps as he rushed to the courtyard.

'It burns, lord, it burns,' a guard whimpered, white-faced.

Saddha Tissa pushed the man aside. 'Ho! A horse! Hurry. What burns so fiercely? Send the men to the Abhaya Wewa. Form water lines!' He found himself roaring as the sound of bursting wood, of the crackling of stones exploding amidst the firestorm that bent the trees and sprayed the ground with spatters of angry red. Jets of orange smoke leaped high and there were monks—monks scurrying to safety, their faces bathed in sweat, their eyes large and pained. 'The Brazen Palace, sire! It burns and the fire demons devour it.'

All it needed was an overturned lamp. The clear oil had

run in a snaking rivulet to the rich curtains that surrounded the small central chamber of the throne. Desperately, the monks had dragged down the flaming cloths but the small chamber grew fiercely hot while the fire leaped angrily from wooden rods to wooden ceiling. The fumes from the heavy material choked them and they fled to raise the alarm. From the upper rooms, monks rushed down even as the floors burst beneath their feet and the wooden steps curled grotesquely. By the time the soldiers, every guard, every man within the citadel had rushed to the water lines, the Brazen Palace had become a roaring tower of flame. The carts rushed water to those at the fringes of the inferno. The entire city was awake, and the screams of women and children pierced the air. It was no use.

Saddha Tissa watched, as in a trance, as this marvel his brother had so lovingly caused to be built, collapsed. Even the stone pillars smoked like giant joss sticks. He groaned. How cruel could things get. He saw his son's face, reddened in the fury of the fire. The trees blackened, and the wind rose to scatter the hot ashes, and the leaves whipped in a blizzard of black. 'We will build it up again,' he said woodenly.

The sounds of the havoc died. People stood silent, listening to the death rattle of something that was so very precious, too glorious to ever die. It had been as a heavenly mansion in life. Death and this fiery consummation was unthinkable. Even as the debris smoked and hissed and burst like orange and scarlet bulbs and growled sharply, many turned away, their faces grimy, their hair and clothes filled with smoke. They returned to their homes like mourners from a cemetery. With bowed heads, hundreds of monks filed past to the Maha Vihara. Their palace, the palace of the heavens, was no more.

Carl Muller

Thulathanaka knew that he would not ask to return to Ruhuna again. He had seen—was it fear?—in his father's eyes. Saddha Tissa—Tissa of the Faith—the king who keeps the faith. Suddenly he could see it all so clearly. His father's faith was the keeping of faith to his brother. Even the monks demanded it of him. All that was expected of him was that he continue to work and die as Duttha Gamani had done. Complete your brother's work...rule as he did...so monstrous an imposition!

How long could his father go on, a pale shadow of his brother? Not long. Just eighteen years...and in that time his eldest son grew powerful and ruled the south with an iron hand. Saddha Tissa rebuilt the Brazen Palace and Thulathanaka was angry that his father had to be so—so apologetic, so meek before the monks.

'The palace cannot be raised to nine levels as it was before,' he had said. 'Seven levels are as high as it will be.'

'But its value diminishes, O King.'

Saddha Tissa had not demurred.

'What is this?' Thulathanaka had asked abruptly, 'Is it value that is paramount? Ten times less will it be in value now, but we build on the ordained site and upon the ruins of the former. Is that not understood?'

Saddha Tissa had said, 'You must not speak the way you did to the brotherhood, our son.'

'But father...'

'Hush. Let us do what we can and leave the rest to others who would better us if they have a mind to. We are past caring.' Never had Thulathanaka heard such bitterness in his father's voice. A great wave of love swept over him. 'Your's has been the greater sacrifice, father. I will remain here with you.'

The inscriptions referred to Saddha Tissa as 'Devanampiya

Maharaja Gamani Tissa'—a maharaja who could not, could never be himself. All over the kingdom, he was merely Duttha Gamani's brother. Nowhere was he talked of without the greater part of such talk being of his brother. When the Sangha spoke too, it was ever of Duttha Gamani and of what he would or could have done. Almost mechanically, Saddha Tissa went on. The *Mahavamsa* tells us that six miles south of Sigiriya, beside a large pool, a *Kaludiyapokuna*,[149] he built the Dakkhinagiri Vihara. Then the Kallakalena, Kalambaka, the Pottangavalika and Velangavitthika, the Dubbalavapitissika and the Matuviharaka. He ordered the construction of a large tank, the Duratissakavapi[150] in Ruhuna, not far from Magama. Who could tell of or understand the pressures that beset his once free spirit? He had to remind his eldest son, and very often too, that he was maharaja, holding sway over the south as well as all the land. He had to also remind the Sangha, the people, that the Buddha had made sacred the whole island—north to south, east to west. Had not the Buddha sat with the brotherhood at Dighavapi? [151]

Thulathanaka was happy to see the old look of happiness in his father's eyes as he turned his attention to the south. The building of the Dighavapi Vihara demanded his journeying to Ruhuna, and he returned, full of the news that Lanja Tissa had also built the beautiful Girikumbhila Vihara and work on the Kandara Vihara[153] has been commissioned in Thulathanaka's name. At every halt on his journey to Dighavapi he asked that a small Vihara be built, then later ordered that viharas rise every yojana of the way.

Thulathanaka also saw a creeping death-pallor in his father's face. 'Too much!' he exclaimed. 'This is too much! What do you wish to do, my father...and prove?

Is it that you think to prove yourself to the people and the monks?'

Saddha Tissa looked away. Yes…what *was* he doing? Was he trying to show the land that he was another, even greater king than his brother? 'We are tired,' he said hoarsely.

Thulathanaka went away, shaking his head.

Eighteen years…In 59 BC Saddha Tissa died. The *Mahavamsa* tells us that, having accomplished so many works of merit, he was reborn among the Tusita gods. Thulathanaka, grieving, thought, 'He was so happy to die. He welcomed the release.'

The astrologers were concerned. 'It is the end of a period,' they said, 'and uncertainty now hangs over the land like a cloud.' They shook their heads.

In Ruhuna, Lanja Tissa told his ministers: 'Look ye upon us. Before you stands the maharaja! Prepare the way for our ceremonial entry to the holy city, for there will we sit in, adorn the throne of the lion!'

The path of tradition has always determined kingship and the law of sucession. Many and varied were the terms used, and one would think them too grandiose for so small an island. Kings were maharajas and Rajadhirajas, Mahipati and Malapalas, Dharanipati, Narapati, Naradhipa and Naradhinatha. Some were expressed as 'Ruler of the Earth', etc. The queens were Mahesi—chief consorts—as there were the concubines as well, and it was only the sons of Mahesi's who had the right to succession. In some cases, there were two Mahesis[153] although there was a difference in rank. The sons and daughters of the reigning king were Rajaputta (son) and Rajaputti (daughter) and the princes were Adipada, the princesses, Rajini. The eldest son was also Yuvaraja. When a son ascends to the throne, the title of Adipada lapses and, as has been noted, the eldest prince—the one nearest to the throne—is also Maha Adipada, and closely associated with Yuvaraja, the successor.

In the case of Lanja Tissa and Thulathanaka, a situation developed that broke with tradition. The monks of Anuradhapura, together with the wise men and elders, insisted that Thulathanaka, younger son, be consecrated Uparaja—a solemn investiture that would make him as king. He becomes the legitimate heir.

It was the rule that the next youngest brother succeed the king on the throne and, if there was no brother, the eldest son of the eldest brother. Lanja Tissa had no doubts that he would be king of all Lanka. He would wait out the period of mourning and go in state for the funeral ceremonies. He was a proud man. He would then return to Ruhuna and await the coming of the chieftains, the high priests, the statesmen, the elders, the ministers of his father's palace. Surely, they would come...and surely would they say, 'Be thou king,' and surely would they bear him away in great pomp. Lanja Tissa wanted this. It would be such a grand spectacle: horses, palanquins, elephants, the outriders of Ruhuna, the cohorts of guards, the standards and banners, the floats, the platforms that would be erected, bedecked with garlands. He would go in state—king of all Lanka!

When the riders came, he could not believe what they had to say. In Anuradhapura, Thulathanaka had been consecrated king!

He snarled and his eyes flashed. With an oath, he summoned his *senapati*[154] and the *mahalekha*.[155]

Carl Muller

'Write!' he said. 'Write that our worthless brother read what we say! Say that within two moons we march in battle order to the kingdom of our father. Say that he must receive us as rightful ruler of all Lanka and that he will give us that which is rightfully ours. Write that should he oppose us, his head will be impaled on the walls!'

To the senapati he had but one command: 'Ready the forces! We will make the Rajarata know the might of the Dakkhinadesa!'[156]

It was the end of peace.

LESSONS UNLEARNED

EVEN AS THE GREAT ARMY OF LANJA TISSA SWEPT BESIDE THE FLOW of the Mahaweli River, leaving the kingdom of Ruhuna behind it, Thulathanaka stood at the outer door of the palace, a look of helplessness on his face. What had he inherited, and was this a boon or a curse? So much had gone into the raising of this city. He could stand at his door and know how ordered, how positively geometric in design it all was. Great Buddhist monasteries stood around the citadel and, around them, the tanks and villages. Like a broad hem around it all were the scrubland and forests, and in them were the hermitages.

There were the streets beside which stood the dwellings of the nobles and wealthy businessmen, as well as the enclaves of the foreigners...and the high walls all around. Everything was so precise, he thought, and yet, how often had the city been breached and the walls made to echo to the screams and roars of offenders, of defenders and the thunder of battle elephants. Hadn't his own great uncle marched up to these walls, killed the wily Elara? This city stood as a challenge, even a magnet to the forces without. It could never really drop its guard...but yet, since times he could recall, the open plains drew enemies with ferocious persistence.

Thulathanaka sighed. How unlike Ruhuna where sea and mountains held the kingdom secure. Would it not make a difference if this city were ringed with steel? But it was ringed with great monasteries, tanks, villages, fields, and places of solitude and meditation. His brother would have no real difficulty storming the kingdom. And could he be driven back? A chilly finger seemed to trace up his spine and he gripped the rail outside the door. Seneviratna[157] has given us a concise description of Anuradhapura in which he says it can be 'categorized basically under different zones or entourages'. The *Athul Nuwara*[158] was half-a-mile square and held the Temple of the Tooth Relic of the Buddha.[159]

The five major monasteries stood around the citadel—the Maha Vihara to the south, the Jetavana Vihara to the east, the Abhayagiri Vihara to the north, the Dakkhina Vihara to the south-west, and the Mirisavati Vihara to the west.

Around these, in the next square area, lay the tanks and the agricultural population that, as Seneviratna says, saw to the requirements of the community of monks. Five reservoirs—the Tissa Wewa, Nuwara Wewa, Abhaya Wewa,[160] the Bulankulama Wewa and the Puliyankulama Wewa—supplied the water to the city and the fields and, as we know, the Tissa Wewa also served the ritual needs of the monks and the king.

The next great square held the scrub and forests, even swamps as well as many small yet picturesque dwellings of the meditative monks and ascetics. The forest-dwelling and cave-dwelling monks were the *vanavasin*s, and their hermitages included the Vessagiri, the Meghagiri,[161] the Paccinarama, Toluvila, Paccina Tissa Pabbata, the Pabbarama,[162] the Asokarama,[163] the Vijayarama and the Uttara Meghagiri Vihara.[164]

With a gesture of impatience, Thulathanaka stepped across the warm stone courtyard to where, honour-guarded by crouching stone lions, a sanded path led to the walls. Ringed by monastic buildings, their gardens and paths aflame with the yellow-robed monks, the city was surely one of much magnificence. The Mahaweli Vidiya[165] was agleam with rosy gravel in the morning sun as were the broader Singuruvak and Candaravanka Vidiyas. And even as the cries of the carters rose and the bazaars rang and the wheels of chariots whirred their songs, Thulathanaka's frown did not leave his face. The administrative heart of his kingdom seemed to stop right here—at these walls. Encircling him was the ritual city, wave upon wave of the most beautiful temples, dagabas, relic houses, monasteries and places of Buddhist learning. Yes...the people, the tanks, the temples. But how could any of these protect the citadel? Within the city were 123,000 people. The fields seemed to stretch interminably and the people sang their songs and washed their clothes upon the rocks of the channels, led their cattle to graze, melted in and out of the temples, carried their offerings of flowers and lit their lamps.

'It all seems so good,' Thulathanaka muttered, 'and now my brother comes. He seeks me! Hah! Who will tell these peaceful peple that he comes to lay bloody hands upon them?' He raised a hand to his eyes. There were the burial grounds, the villages of the outcastes and scavengers. He thought of Prince Saliya and again a sense of unease possessed him. Was not Saliya raised to be king? As he

Carl Muller

turned away, he thought: 'What trick of fate placed me on the throne...was it that I must die?'

A man stood on the old Aritthagiri road where the track to Anuradhapura skirted the forbidding Ritigala Mountain. He stood alone and in his hand was a sword. His dark hair, unknotted, tumbled greasily to his shoulders and his lithe, bare body seemed to shine in the sun. Lanja Tissa, on his war elephant, scowled. His army had taken the longer, easier route, having rounded Pulatthinagara[166] to approach the city from the south-east. In three hours, his forces would meet the road from Mihintale and then the final furious rush into Anuradhapura.

'Who is he? What does he want, standing with weapon bared in our way?' he growled. As if in reply, the man tossed his head, shaking his hair, and raised his sword threateningly. 'Turn back!' he roared. 'Would you march upon my father's kingdom?'

The commander checked his horse. 'A mad man, surely, O King.'

'What! Does he say he is a prince? Mow him down!'

A woman, her breasts uncovered, broke out of the heavy shrubs that reared over the rocks. She ran to the man, seized his arm, tried to pull him away. Her face was half-hidden in the wildness of her hair and even as she implored, the man freed himself and pushed her to the side of the road. Her wail of despair rose in the air.

'Uncovered she comes to take the mad man away. They are of lowly birth, sire,' the commander said.

Lanja Tissa sneered. 'This is how my cowardly brother guards his realm! With outcastes! Ride them down. Ho! Archers, unleash your bolts!'

There was time enough to kill. As the archers raised their bows, many thought that the mad man would flee, but he stood defiant, eyes blazing, roaring his cotempt. The arrows seemed to bristle in his body as he quivered and clawed at the fires that burst within him.

The screams of the woman became frenzied as she rushed out to fall upon the man. 'You have killed him! Does it take an army to kill one man! True king did you kill! You, the false one!'

An arrow pierced her back as she bent over, crooning piteously, raising the head of the man whose eyes were dead. Blood trickled from the side of his mouth and his jaw lay slack. With a gasp, the woman fell upon him and another arrow made its vicious way into her neck.

'Mad men, mad women…eaters of dead meat, we warrant. Let the elephants grind them into the earth!' Lanja Tissa snarled. 'Forward!'

Among the trees, a pale-faced man sped away to the mountains. He sobbed as he ran. How would he tell the village that they were dead? Better he die rather than carry the awful news, but he ran and minded not the brambles he leaped over. Tonight would all the settlements by the river weep…and even as they did, even as the ageing parents of Asokamala Devi lay aswoon, their pain too hard to bear, the invaders reached the walls, fiercely slaughtering all who stood before them.

They poured through the gates and the elephants charged the doors and ran amok among the outhouses, wrecking and tearing down walls and causing pillars to crumble. It was a havoc so brief to be almost unreal. Among the dead lay Thulathanaka, his young face still wearing the frown of the morning, his chest split open.

The city was as a tomb. In their homes, people cowered

Carl Muller

and in the monasteries, monks held up their hands in consternation. In the Thuparama, the brotherhood struck their breasts silently, lips moving in prayer. Had they made a mistake? They had consecrated the younger prince, ignoring the elder. Now had the elder come among them and he had raged and slain his brother and declared himself king. They retired to their cells. No bells were sounded. The lamps burned low and in the city rose the sound of a victorious roaring and southerners ranged the streets and the death drums were everywhere.

So did Saliya and his chandala wife die on the Aritthagiri road. A prince to the end surely, for he alone stood in the way of Lanja Tissa's avenging army. Asokamala Devi knew that her prince would die. She had wept as she stumbled behind him, pleading that he return home. She had crouched among the rearing shrub, helpless as the arrows whistled. She could do nothing, but she could die with her lord. It was many moons later that the people of Anuradhapura learnt of the tragedy and, dull-eyed, they nodded and went indoors to light a stick of incense at their tiny altars. What did it matter? In truth, nothing really mattered. Duttha Gamani had died. Vihara Maha Devi was dead. Saddha Tissa was dead. Prince Saliya was dead and his shame had died with him. Now the sons of Saddha Tissa would sit in turn upon the throne. Already one had killed the other and more waited their turn in Ruhuna.

The evil had been unleashed once again. Why could not Ruhuna confine itself to Ruhuna? Who could understand this lust for power? They shook their heads. Always, they knew, when Sihala fought Sihala, the Damilas rose.

Would the Sihala never learn from the lessons of the past?

A CAULDRON OF KINGS

MORE THAN A CENTURY AGO, HENRY W. CAVE, A MEMBER OF THE Royal Asiatic Society, wrote a glowing book: *The Ruined Cities of Ceylon* (London, 1904). It would be well to offer an extract from this book if only to set the atmosphere, the very mood of this chapter. On the one hand we have Anuradhapura, a mighty city—a city that rose because of the social order that made for precision and progress and a people who held fast to the laid-out order and made industry their watchword. As Cave pointed out:

> The order and contentment prevailing amongst the rural population surprise us no less than the perfection of method in the operation of agriculture. These people work to feed not only themselves but also the millions inhabiting the vast cities...A life of idleness would not be possible even were it desired. The common folk, are desired by a despotic monarch, to cultivate the land. This coercion is, however, the secret of their wealth and happiness, for the habits thus imposed upon them from without, render their country healthy and fertile, while their simple home life, undisturbed by care or ambition, favours the increase of population. Throughout the country, great blocks of solid gneiss...are engraved with injunctions for the maintenance

of the system of cultivation and of unity and concord among the people.

It may be well to ponder on the quoted text. Slab inscriptions that spelt out how life should be lived...the need for unity and concord. This was a Lanka that may have danced to the tune of its kings, but deep-seated was the knowledge that the land called for the efforts of all. The people of old Lanka were not in any way different from the millions that people Sri Lanka today, yet there are now, too many different drums being beaten, and if the writer may make a tongue-in-cheek observation, should anyone raise an engraved slab today, calling for an adherence to a system of concord and unity, such slab would soon be defaced with garish posters proclaiming such manifestations as 'Kung-fu Classes' and the latest blood-daubed movie and the news that some local Squeers is offering tuition in botany and advanced mathematics!

And yet, as glorious as the capital city of Anuradhapura was, so few were there who ruled as they were expected to. Lanja Tissa ruled for three years with feelings of deep resentment. The monks had slighted him. 'No,' he growled. 'They did not decide according to age!' But he grew more bewildered, more fretful, when he realized how the people regarded him. It was then that he realized the real truth of the kingdom, the very lion seat that was his. Yes...kings would come and go...yes, he could hold power with the sword, make of his hands mailed fists...but there, in the fields, among the gardens scented with jasmine, in each maiden's hands clasped in salutation before the temples, in the gently breathing bosoms of every tank... what a fool he had been! There lay the eternal equation: the temple, the village, the tank. That was the land's true glory...Wrapping a shawl around his neck, he strode to the Maha Vihara.

It is perhaps the Hindu sociocultural concepts that made many of Lanka's kings consider themselves near-divine. It was the nature of the Brahmanistic structure of society that made these kings grow so sure of themselves: so sure that they could not merely be the defenders of the faith but that they could give offence to the faith as well. Also there was the peculiar Hindu notion of 'heredity both of blood and culture'.[167]

What Lanja Tissa did not wish to admit to was that he had rejected the will of the Sangha and that he had actually 'invaded' the kingdom. Also, he did not wish to admit to the fact that the king was conceived to be powerful only when he upheld dhamma—the law. Of course, the Brahmana texts tell us that dhamma, too, was created by Brahma when he found that the kingship was not powerful enough in itself. It tended to invest kings with 'divine right' and, as we have seen, this right was, more often than not, might.

What Lanja Tissa did not see was the new concept of dhamma—when the Buddha radically transformed the Brahmanistic concepts. In fact, as Radhakrishnan points out,[168] the Buddha objected to the identification of dhamma with any being outside of Nature.

What was the true face of Lanka? With the Buddha dhamma steeped in the hearts of the people, the real land was not as the king would have supposed it to be—the throne and the citadel. No, it was (and the writer likes to think it must always be), the temple, village and tank. The people of old came to accept this new socio-morality and

Carl Muller

their teachers and guides were the monks. And, if the king turns away from the Sangha, who would instruct him? How would such a king be a truly ideal monarch? What glory lay in the village! There was the *gama* with its rice fields, garden land and families usually of one kinship.[169] There was the *nigama*—a market town and meeting place of trade routes.[170] There was the *patungama*, an urbanized settlement, usually coastal and with a small harbour. Mahatittha[171] and Gokonna[172] were patungamas.[173] Finally, the *pura* or *nagara*—the city, the seat of government.

All this depended on water, and hence the tanks that gave the gamas life, and the temples that told this life how to live. How then could anyone explain or resign himself to the fact that the king and the monks acted apart? If there was no close connection between the Sangha and the monarchy, how could state and society function as one?

Buddhism had always exerted a profound influence on the institution of kingship. What could the people now say of their king? They could not understand any man, any king, who scorned the brotherhood. Such a king could not truly be a king and such a man no man at all. Let Devendra[174] say it:

> ...these people are heir to an amazing culture. One sees it in...waterworks, reservoirs, extending beyond a surface coverage of four thousand five hundred acres...they live upon a small land in a corner of Asia...they led their own life from about the time Rome was founded...their way of life marked out by the tank which nourished their rice, the food of today as it was of the countless yesterdays in the memories of men.'

Lanja Tissa entered the holy premises on foot, his shawl on his head, his sandals hastily kicked off his feet. The monks listened, their eyes slightly closed. They accepted that humility did not sit easily on this man and knew that he had come, not to be humble but to make atonement in his own way.

'We have decided, O monks, that three terraces be built that offerings of flowers be made at the great Cetiya.'

The monks listened, silent.

'We have also seen how the land dips and remains uneven between the Thuparama and the Maha Thupa.[175] This makes it difficult for the worshippers who must make their visits. We will heap the earth in order that the floor be levelled.'

The monks inclined their heads, remained silent.

'It is that we fear we have not given enough thought to the holy edifices, O monks. Would you give us your blessing on this we wish to do?'

An old monk raised a hand. 'It pleases us that the king has soft words for the brotherhood. Will you not, even now, say that it was within our right to wish your younger brother to be king? The quality of kingship is one that few can possess; yet many wish to sit upon the throne. When spurred by wrong reason and anger and—yes, pride—what kind of king would such be? For many moons have the holy places been neglected. Is it that the king has come to know himself after so long a time?'

'That we have...and much have we to do.'

'It would be necessary to cover the thupa in the Thuparama with a mantle of stone.'

'That, too, will we do. And a small thupa to the south-west which will stand as a symbol of our renewed faith. We will call it the Digathupa...and a special hall for the brotherhood...'

In the settlements beyond the rivers, the songs of the gatherers serenaded the skies, and ease stretched in the souls and smiles of a more contented people. All was well. The king and the Sangha were as one. See...the king mantles the thupa on the high rocks of the Missaka Mountain...and there rises the Cetiya Vihara. What a stirring consecration is to be conducted. It will be called the festival of the Girikumbhila[176]...and see...there rises the Aritha Vihara beside the Aritthapabbata and also the Kunjarahinaka Vihara...It was in 50 BC that Lanja Tissa died, to be succeeded by his younger brother Khallata Naga. The new king continued the work of merit. He wished, like his brother, like so many other kings, to leave a legacy in stone. He raised thirty-two beautiful dwelling places around the Brazen Palace for the monks, and built an outer wall around the Ruvanweliseya, strewing the enclosure with fine sand mined from the Kadambanadi Oya.[177] All over the land the people lived their quiet lives, content in the thought that their king worked tirelessly for the faith. It was very necessary that monarch and Sangha so meet. It gave them a sense of order and well-being. None could accept that the comfort of the nation could be in jeopardy as long as the king occupied himself in the glorification of the faith, but he failed to see the treachery spawned within his walls.

Troop commander Kammakarattaka was a surly man, acclaimed as a brutal warrior and of ferocious mien. He had little use for the loyalty of his men, nor had he any use for the love and loyalty of his wife and sons. He had no use for myth, legend, or the wondrous tales spun by the monks who upheld their views with stories of marvellous beings, miracles and the passage of the gods.

No one saw beneath the cruelty of his manner—the way he beat his wife, the way he trod on his men, the hard practical man who told himself that no divinity could dabble with the lives of men. He had one friend, surprisingly: a learned man who had spent many years in a mountain retreat and who had convinced himself that man needs to strip away the layers of myth to find the kernel that reposes in his own soul. Kammakarattaka would listen to him, a scowl on his face, for he was wont to scowl even in concentration.

'You are wiser than those old fools who pretend to advise the court,' he would say. 'Why do you not proclaim yourself? Assuredly would you be my adviser were I king.'

The scholar raised an eyebrow. 'A scowling king? Why are you possessed of such rage. Surely there are things that please you...'

'What can please me? Look you, the troops are grown fat and lazy and many spend time in their village fields and care not for barrack life. The horse guards are no more on their steeds. There is naught but empty show. Every day the palace guards strut the walls and bastions and ogle the women in the streets. The royal treasury is plundered at every whim of the king. What does he do? He is a builder! A mason to the monks! That's what he is. Not once has it been told of or heard that the bhikkhus tell the king to desist. "I will build this and this," he says and the monks beam their approval.'

The scholar nodded. 'Yes, there is some truth in that, yet it is now considered a kingly duty.'

'Duty! The king's first duty is to the people. All this spinning and weaving of fanciful tales...I tell you, the monks lead the king by the nose.'

'You may be right again, commander, but who can talk of reform when anger burns within him? Who will listen to such? Is it not so that you are shunned and feared? No, listen…I see much in you, but you marry impatience with violence and disbelief with scorn. Let me explain. Talk to anyone in the land. Ask them about the devas and the king of the devas. They believe, do they not? Yet, here in this city, do you find any place where the devas are worshipped? And this king of the devas? Who is he? The god Sakkra, it is said. No edifice is raised here in his honour.'

'I grant you that, but the belief in these beings or creatures cannot be effaced.'

'Ah yes, the monks again. They tell the tales. You see what is being done, don't you? Why is it, one may ask, if the Buddha insisted that there are no other beings superior to man, the monks keep alive the stories of these gods and devas?'

'To fool us! That's what they do. And to fool the king!'

'Exactly, my fine fellow. When rafts of devas and devatas are created to range the earth and the skies, what are men to do? This Sakkra is said to have a thousand eyes. Our foolish people take it all so literally, do they not?'

'Thousand eyes! If I had five hundred of my men ranging the land, reporting to me of all they see, then my eyes too will be a thousand.'

'Ah, you have a sharp mind. Perhaps you are right…of course you are right. Spies, not eyes. You have rude wisdom, Kammakarattaka. Shall I tell you what you need?

'Need? What?'

'Transform the boiling iron of your anger into cold steel.'

'What does that mean?

'It means that you act with cold determination and not with blazing emotion. Think of what we have spoken. When a man accepts that there are no gods and devas and all those other packs of mythological creatures, that man is free to choose greatness by the means he uses best. Free of the burdens the monks heap on him. But put aside the anger that bubbles within you. Freeze it. Encase it in ice. Cold cruelty is the best, yet vilest in form. But it makes you think and plan and not overheat your brain. Yes, you will make a viper-eyed leader of men.' [178]

When Kammakarattaka went to his king, he did not humble himself. His hand flew to his sword and before the horrified eyes of officials and slaves he held the point of his weapon at Khallata Naga's throat. 'Rise! Come down from that lion seat!' he snarled, 'Or this sword will run its way through you!'

There was a rush for the doors and the sound of the alarm and the clatter of men, but the troops that swept in checked themselves. Their commander—their hated commander! But they feared him. He had dragged the king off the throne and sat in it himself and a strong hand held the king around the neck, bending his body against the hard arm of the seat where a bronze lion's head bit into the king's spine. The sword lay across the stricken man's belly.

Outside, horsemen sped to the eastern palace where the king's younger brother Vatta Gamini was, and who had come to the kingdom to pay his respects and visit the holy places.

'Who is this traitor!' he roared. 'What? The troop commander? And what do the troops do?' With trembling hands he seized sword and pike and shouted for his men. 'Is my brother dead?'

'He is held at sword point, lord. Kammakarattaka occupies the throne.'

When Vatta Gamini stormed the hall, fighting broke

Carl Muller

out between his men and the king's troops. With an oath, Kammakarattaka slashed wide Khallata Naga's belly, pushed the corpse away. Blood jetted as it arched and fountained, and with reddened sword Khammakarattaka leaped to meet the lunging Vatta Gamini. They tumbled down the steps together, lay clawing at each other in a warm bloodslick. Vatta Gamini flung aside his sword, snatched a dagger from his waist and buried it in his adversary, again and again. The king's troops fled in disarray and horrified courtiers watched Vatta Gamini's arm pumping—rising, falling. When he finally kicked himself free, Kammakarattaka's body was a tattered sieve.

'Twenty-three times,' the captain of the guard muttered. 'That many times did the dagger cleave the flesh.'

Chamberlain and slaves helped Vatta Gamini to the baths and Khallata Naga's queen, Anula Devi, embraced her little son, Mahaculika, and wailed loudly. 'O brother of my king, what will we do?'

Vatta Gamini placed a hand on her shoulder. 'Have we not a prince, your son and my nephew, to look after? Ho there! Let a messenger carry our greetings to the monks. Say that we, Vatta Gamini, take our brother's throne, his queen and his son. Say that we take the place of the father.'

'A *pitiraja*,' [179] said the high priest. 'It is well. For long have we not had such as this. Let the king be told that we will perform the ritual of purification. The seat of the lion has been defiled.'

The scholar in his retreat sat cross-legged, staring at the trees, the sun dapples, the stirring leaves. 'Such a fool you were,' he said to himself. 'Had you but waited...but no, you raged too much and your blind anger was your undoing.' He shook his head. 'I must go away to Ruhuna—find another disgruntled one...'

The scholar, Parumaka, was fair-skinned and did not don the robes of the Brahmin. He wore no sacred ash on his forehead. His staff was of knotted wood. In his retreat were no altars, no couch. When he walked out, he carried nothing but his staff, and the Vijithapura road[180] was hot and patchy with thorn creepers. He knew the tracks. He spent the night at Kalaha-Nagara[181] where the Amban and Mahaweli Rivers united. The next day he came to the Dola Mountain[182] and followed the rocky passes to the south.

In Ruhuna, he found it easy to find the young Brahmin, Tissa. 'No, rise not, for I have much to say. The time is upon us. Across the water a Damila army readies to sail. For the Sihala it is now a time of confusion and uncertainty. Kings come and go, and none die in peace. It is the time I told you of, O Tissa.'

'It is the same in this realm,' said Tissa. 'I had thought that perhaps I should rise up and take this southern kingdom.'

'Yes, that is a bold plan—but it is Anuradhapura that must totter. This Vatta Gamini is a fearless man, but he is also plagued by uncertainty. After Kammakarattaka, he fears his own troops. Everywhere in the ranks are charges of traitor levelled and many are sentenced to death each day. That is good—and there is the greed of the courtiers as well. They seek the lands of those they denounce. Tell me, how many of your clan have you?'

'Many...ah, but I have not been idle. Since the death of Duttha Gamani have I been in preparation.'

'You have done well. A goodly force, I presume.'

Carl Muller

'Two thousand, well armed. Much more if I were to count those in the border villages.'

Parumaka was pleased. 'Do you then move out. Let not the city know of the movements of your men. They should leave in small groups, on horseback or in carts and keep their arms hidden. In the jungles, two miles to the north of the Missaka Mountain must they assemble. It is the district of Gangaraji, at the village beside the Pavarasan tank which is given to the Brahmins. Make that your post.'

'This Damila force you tell of...it will march on the capital, will it not? Is it that we join them?'

Purumaka laughed. 'We do not, for these Damilas are renegades. They come to plunder. When they have stripped the city, taken what women they wish, they will leave. But we await their landing, for there are those of the north who will also carry their threats to Vatta Gamini. What you will do is also convey your own threats. What will the king do? Will he fight on two fronts with an army he cannot trust? He will also think you Tissa, of Ruhuna—a Sihala.'

'Yes, I see what you plan. Truly, you are a master of intrigue.'

A cauldron of kings...let us consider the sorry pass this island was reduced to from 101 to 59 BC—for forty-two years after the defeat of Elara, Lanka came to know what stability was. Those were the years of peace and high endeavour. Then came the sons of Saddha Tissa and, as has been recorded, they were all fated to hold power, each for a little time only. Thulathanaka ruled for a year and ten days, until his elder brother Lanja Tissa stormed the city. The latter sat on the Lion Throne for nine years and fifteen days...and he was succeeded by his brother

Khallata Naga who ruled, quite blindly, for six years. His troop commander then seized the throne—a few short hours, true, but would history consider him a king for a day? It was then Vatta Gamini's turn—and his time, too, was short. Within five months, he had to learn of a twin threat: the rebel Tissa from Ruhuna who demanded that he give over the royal parasol of authority, and the demands of seven Damila warriors who landed with their army at Mahatittha.[183]

Vatta Gamini had his problems, having accepted the role of Pitiraja. He wished to do battle with the Damilas, but he also carried with him, in his chariot, his two queens—his own queen, Soma Devi, and the wife of his brother, Anula Devi. 'She must be protected,' he told his queen, for Anula Devi carried a child—his child. He also took with him his own son, Maha Naga, and the son of Anula Devi, Mahacula. A strange way to prepare for and go to battle? Who can say what determined the king to act the way he did. In truth, he was tormented with doubts. Would his guardsmen slaughter Anula Devi and her son? And, in the bloodletting, would they kill his own queen and prince? Soma Devi was strikingly beautiful, the southern blood rich in her veins.

The *Mahavamsa* tells us that Vatta Gamini was a wily man. When he received the demands of Tissa as well as that of the Damilas, he sent a bearer to Tissa, offering him the kingdom if Tissa would first do battle with and rout the Damilas. It bought Vatta Gamini time.

Tissa pitched his men against the Damilas and lost. He and his troops were slain at the borders of the forest of Tumbara-Kandara, and the triumphant Damilas bore down on the city. As the *Mahavamsa* says:

In a battle near Kolambalaka,[184] the king was vanquished...
as a nigantha[185] named Giri saw him take flight, he cried

out loudly, 'The great black lion is fleeing'...He took Anula Devi with him, who was with child...and Mahacula also, and his son, the prince Maha Naga...but to lighten the car, the king gave to Soma Devi his splendid diadem jewel and let her, with her own consent, descend from the car.

In his flight, he could not take with him a precious relic—the alms bowl of the Buddha.[186]

Vatta Gamini and his family went into hiding. They moved from the Vassagiri forest to Silasobbhakandaka[187] and then to Mutuvelanga near Samagalla[188] and lived in the home of the attendant of the thera Kuppikkala Maha Tissa. It would be fifteen years before he would return to the lion seat. Anuradhapura was once again in the hands of the Damilas!

Endnotes

The Right To Love

1. *Diospyros embryopteris*—A native tree of India, Sri Lanka and Malaysia. The unripe fruits are used for tanning fishing nets. It is a useful shade tree in semi-dry regions.
2. As said in *Kuttanimatam* and *Kathakautukam.*
3. The idea.
4. Sexual excitement.
5. John Muir: *Original Sanskrit Texts,* Vol. 2, London, 1868–70.
6. Emerson Tennent: *Ceylon,* Vol. 2, London, 1860.
7. John Davy: *An Account of the Interior of Ceylon,* London, 1821.
8. References are found in Fustel de Coulanges: *The Ancient City,* Boston 1874; W.E. Heam: *The Aryan Household,* London 1879; and J.D. Mayne: *A Treatise on Hindu Law and Marriage,* Madras, 1888.
9. John Muir: *Religion and Moral Sentiments Metrically Rendered from Sanskrit,* London, 1890.
10. Monier Williams: *Buddhism in its Connexion with Brahminism and Hinduism,* London, 1890.

11. Rhys Davids: *Lectures on the Origin and Growth of Religion as Illustrated by Some Points in the History of Buddhism [The Hibbert Lectures, 1881]*, London, 1881.

12. Nandasena Ratnapala: *Folklore of Sri Lanka,* Colombo, 1991.

13. Dowry is given in kind and cash and always before assembled relatives. This is done on the day of the *Namdima*—the publication of banns—or on the day of the marriage. Dowry from the bride's side is always given to the bridegroom or one of his relatives.

14. Taboo.

15. The Sinhalese believe that blood is the staple food of the Yakas, demons and other evil spirits. These demons infest one who bleeds and this is the cause of kili—the connection between blood and demons. It is for this reason that blood is offered (usually the blood of a cockerel) in ceremonies to propitiate a demon. The kili that comes with the rupture of the hymen is believed to last from three to seven days. It is necessary for the woman to take the necessary precautions since she is impure and will remain impure under the sinister influence of kili.

A Miracle In The Making

16. Terraces.

17. According to Manu, the kahapana was a copper coin, 80 gunjas in weight where a gunja is 1.8 grains. In medieval Lanka, however, the kahapana was a gold coin. (See H.W. Codrington: *Ceylon Coins and Currency,* Colombo, 1924.)

18. The *Mahavamsa* tells of how Mahinda, priest-son of Emperor Asoka of India, pointed to this site and told King Devanampiya Tissa: 'Thus, O king, this is a spot consecrated by the four preceding Buddhas. On this spot, maharaja, there will hereafter stand a dagaba to serve as a shrine of *dona* of sacred

relics obtained from Buddha's body...' ('shrine of dona' is the vessel in which relics are measured). The chronicle also says that the Buddha himself foretold the enshrinement of a dona of his corporeal relics in the great thupa.

19. A capacity measure of about 700 handfuls.

20. This compass, as Smither tells us in *Architectural Remains, Anuradhapura, Sri Lanka* (Colombo, 1894), was a trammel composed of many united lengths of straight upright bars with a pivot at one end and a tracer at the other. The pivot point was worked into a socket of brass and silver plates.

21. It must be noted that the present principal entrance to the Ruwanveliseya is towards the east.

22. The hymn of joy which the Buddha uttered at the moment of attaining Buddhahood.

23. This could be white dolomite which has the colour of uncooked meat fat. Such stones have been found in many excavated relic chambers in Sri Lanka.

24. Swan.

25. The making of such a statue will imply that the indigenous artisan community was already well advanced by this time, but from whose workshops no prior works have survived. It is obvious that Duttha Gamani would not have wished the artisans to carry forward their art and make it available to other temples and dagabas, since he wished his design for the Maha Thupa to be unique. Such art, then, was not allowed to flower. Perhaps this is why the first carbon-14-dated Lankan images of the Buddha, that are life-sized sculptures, are from the first century AD.

26. This tells how well Hindu imagery blended with the Buddhist in those times.

27. Pancasikha is the equivalent of Hinduism's Sarasvati. He plays to please Sakkha and is always accompanied by is own host of *gandhabba*s (Sanskrit *gandharva*) or divine musicians. It is interesting to note that this same word, 'gandharva', was

used for the Greek province of West Asia, now Afghanistan. We must remember the Greek penchant for music which may give rise to a historical basis for this popular myth.

28. Mara (death) is the Buddhistic counterpart of Shiva in his destructive aspect. Certain texts have it that Mara has a thousand arms. He is always accompanied by legions of evil spirits and his beautiful daughters who are well versed in the arts of the seductress and the temptress. As has been told in *Children of the Lion*, the combined efforts of Mara and his forces failed to deter the Buddha from attaining enlightenment.

29. These kings are also the Lokapala—the guardians of the world, with Dhatarattha in the north, Virulha in the south, Virupakkha in the west and Vessavana in the east.

30. These devas are called *weerupakkho*.

31. The Wheel of the doctrine—a sacred symbol of the Buddhists. In *Journal of the Royal Asiatic Society*, 1886, Robert Sewell suggests that this was originally the sun symbol.

32. The word given is *vijjulata*—streams of lightning—doubtless rendered in jewels or crystal upon the stone to illumine or set off the chamber.

33. Carbon black comes from the soot of carbonized oils. Because a great deal of oil is needed to bind the colour, the drying process is slow. Vermilion is the red pigment of cinnabar and is a colour of great durability. Many earth colours were used by the artists of those times. Lead-tin yellow, a compound of lead and tin oxide was used, while blue, rarely used, came from a basic copper carbonate now called azurite. The Roman writer Pliny called it Caeruleum from which we have the expression 'cerulean blue'. Dark reds were usually drawn from the crushed cochineal insect, while the green came from malachite, a fine, green copper ore that was ground to make the pigment.

34. The *Dipavamsa* gives in detail the dynasties of that age when

the world was new. It was in the beginning of this yugaya that Mahasammata reigned, and with him the kings Roja, Vararoja, Kalyana, and Varakalyana, Uposatha, Mandhatar, Caraka and Upacaraka, Cetiya, Mucala and Mahamucala, Mucalinda, Sagara and Sagaradeva, Bharata, Angirasa, Ruci and Suruci, Patapa and Mahapatapa. There was also Panada and Mahapanada who thera Bhaddaji claimed to be; Sudarsanna, Neru and Accina. All these kings, the sons and princes of Mahasammata, dwelt in Kusavati (later Kusinara—a town of the clan of the Mallas, now in Nepal), Rajagaha (now Rajgir and the old capital of Magadha) and Mithila in the Bengal district of Tirhut. Then followed one hundred kings who dwelt in Pakulu, the last of whom was Arimdana. The *Dipavamsa* lists the following thereafter: fifty-six kings at Ayujjha, the last being Duppasaka; sixty kings at Benares, the last being Ajitajana; 84,000 kings at Kapilanagara, the last being Brahmadatta; thirty-six kings at Hatthipura, the last being Kambalavasabha; thirty-two kings at Ekacakkhu, the last being Purindadeva; twenty-eight kings at Vajira, the last being Sadhina; twenty-two kings at Madhura, the last being Dhammagutta; eighteen kings at Aritthapura, the last being Sitthi; seventeen kings at Indapatta, the last being Brahmadeva; fifteen more kings at Ekacakkhu, the last being Baladatta; fourteen kings at Kosambi, the last being Bhaddadeva; nine kings at Kannagoccha, the last being Naradeva; seven kings at Rajananagara, the last being Mahinda; twelve kings at Campa, the last being Nagadeva; twenty-five kings at Mithila, the last being Buddhadatta; twenty-five kings at Rajagaha, the last being Dipamkara; twelve kings at Taksila, the last being Talissara; twelve kings at Kusinara, the last being Purinda; nine kings at Malitthiya, the last being Sagaradeva. Sagaradeva's son was Makhadeva, whose dynasty of 84,000 reigned at Mithila. The last of these princes was Nemiya, whose son was Kalamjanaka. He was followed by Samamkura, then Asoka, and again a dynasty of

84,000 who reigned at Benares. The last of these was Vijaya who was succeeded by Vijitasena, Dhammasena, Nagasena, Samatha, Disampati, Renu, Kusa, Mahakusa, Navaratha, Dasaratha, Rama, Bilaratha, Cittadassi, Atthadassi, Sujata and Okkaka. Okkamukkha was Okkaka's eldest son while other sons and grandsons were Nipuna, Candima, Candamukkha, Sivisamjaya, Vessantara, Jali, Sihavahana, and Sihassara who counted 82,000 sons and grandsons, Jayasena being the last of them. They were the Sakya kings of Kapilavatthu, the birthplace of Gotama Buddha. Jayasena's son was Sihahanu, his daughter Yasodhara. Sihahanu had five sons and two daughters, while in Devadaha there lived a prince named Devadahasakka who gave his daughter Kaccana to be the first consort of Sihahanu, while his son Anjana took to wife Yasodhara. Anjana had two daughters, Maya and Pajapati, and two sons, Dandapani and Suppabuddha. Of Sihahanu's sons, Suddhodana made Maya and Pajapati his queens, and it is the son of Suddhodana and Maya who became the Buddha Gotama. It was necessary to make this long note if only to show that the thera Bhaddaji, even as he watched the swirling of the waters, was, in a previous life, the ancestor of the master he now followed.

35. In *Children of the Lion* we have given in appendices, the Planes of Existence. The Brahma world consists of the three worlds of the first Jhana Realm—Brahma Paisajja, Brahma Purohita and Maha Brahma, where existence lasts for one-and-five-sixths celestial ages.

The Serpent World

36. The Kolityas were of a tribe related to the Sakyas. As told in *Children of the Lion,* the kingdom of the Koliyas was separated from that of the Sakyas by the river Rohini, and yet this did not deter the coming together of the Sakya prince Siddhartha Gotama and the Koliya princess Yasodhara. The

Sumangalavilasini says that the Koliya capital was Vijagghapajja, but Ramagama or Rajagama is the accepted name.

37. Asoka the Great.

38. The distinct tropical forests found from Kashmir to Nepal and Bhutan. The major species of tree found in the terai is the sal—*Shorea robusta*.

39. Kana rivers.

40. E.J. Thomas: *History of Buddhist Thought*, London, 1953. Kala, the Naga king said to Gotama on the day of his enlightenment:

Even as Krakucchandra goes,
Konakamuni and Kasyapa,
So dost thou go, tatha gacchasi, O great hero,
Buddha today thou become.

41. The Nikaya texts give us much detail about the Nagas. According to the *Naga Samyutta,* there are four types of Nagas: *Andaja Naga,* egg-born—the cobra; *Jalabuja Naga,* womb-born—the human; *Samsedaja Naga,* moisture-born; and *Opapatika Naga,* of spontaneous birth. Ref: *Digha Nikaya,* T.W. Rhys Davids and J.E. Carpenter (eds) (Pali Text Society, London, 1890–1911) and D.D. Kosambi, *An Introduction to the Study of Indian History*, Bombay, 1956. In both Pali and Sanskrit texts, Naga refers to both cobra and elephant, and this is also mentioned in the dictionary of the Pali Text Society as well as in the *Sanskrit-English Dictionary*, Sir M. Monier Williams (ed.), Oxford, 1899. If we consider womb-born, this clearly indicates groups of tribals associated with the Naga cult who existed in India from the earliest times. Kosambi states: 'Naga tribes survive in Assam and Burma. Their demand for autonomy is a considerable source of embarrassment to the new national government today. Other Nagas appeared in history in the northern part of

central India as minor kings who issued a few coins for a brief period, about 150 AD...' In *Gods in Early Buddhism*, Colombo 1974, M.M.J. Marasinghe mentions the possibility of Naga tribes existing in the Gangetic regions during the Buddha's time. The *Mahaparinibbana Sutta* tells us that even in Rajagama, the eighth drona of relics was worshipped by Nagas and that the people of Rajagama were Nagas. The *Samyutta Nikaya* insists that the Nagas always had the Buddha's sympathy. Kosambi adds: 'Who, then, were these Nagas, snake demons and yet human at the same time, evil enough to be destroyed by a specially powerful fire sacrifice and yet whose females could bear legitimate, highly responsible children to Brahmins? The answer can be worked out from extant sources. Apparently, Naga became a generic term for forest aborigines, not necessarily connected or inter-related, who had a cobra totem or worshipped the cobra as so many Indian aborigines (and not only other aborigines) still do. These particular Nagas were in the jungle at the time Kuru-land (one of the sixteen great tribal territories of India from about the seventh century BC) was first settled by Aryans.' Despite all this, no explanation has been found for the 'moisture-bearing Nagas' who, legend has it, emerge from deep waters. Likewise, no explanation has been given for the mysterious manner in which the stupa at Rajagama, that contained the eighth drona of relics, was rebuilt after the great flood. Although there is little evidence, legend has it that the Nagas of Rajagama returned to build the stupa, hoping that in doing so, the urn would be miraculously returned to them. This would account for how, much later, Emperor Asoka found the stupa intact.

42. There is mention in the *Mahavagga* that an ordained bhikkhu was later discovered to be a Naga and was asked to leave the Order.

43. Ornamental archways.

44. An island off Mantai, on the north-east coast.

45. The *Rajavaliya*, B. Gunasekara (ed.), Colombo, 1900, claims that 96 *kotis*—9,600,000 monks, by superhuman powers, came in the air from different lands of India to be present at the sacred festival of depositing the relics. The *Mahavamsa* adds that Sakkha, king of the gods, ordered Vissakamma, the heavenly builder, to adorn the whole island of Lanka in manifold ways.

46. The car or chariot of the state.

47. These horses were specially imported from the Indus country (Sanskrit: *Saindhava*). These horses are of an excellent breed and are much prized. Indian literature makes much mention of them.

48. A port in the northern province.

49. The Malwattu and Kala rivers respectively, Mihintale.

50. Also called Cetaligama, south of Anuradhapura.

51. Also called Dvrammandalakagama, a village near Mihintale.

52. D.H. Rawcliff: *The Psychology of the Occult*, London, 1952. This is referred to as Ascenesthesia and is thought to be a sensation associated with certain types of paranoia. In the ancient Puranas (cf. *Garuda Purana*) it can be brought on by adepts in order to journey into other dimensions free of physical encumbrances.

53. It is seen how serpents are the commonest creatures in mythology. They have featured in the idolatrous worship of the Biblical Jews, and right up to the snake-handling cults of the present day. Serpent worship has been a particular practice in India since prehistoric times, and these old snake cults were assimilated into the religion of the invading Aryans. Even Greek mythology tells of the battle between the gods and serpents, while Egypt had its own snake god; and Japan a multi-headed serpent god; Scandanavia, a giant serpent god; Polynesia, a monster snake; and the Aztecs, the Plumed Serpent. In many regions the snake deity is depicted with its tail in its mouth, thus representing an all-encircling cosmic

force that protects and comforts its followers. Such is the characteristic of the serpent god Da or Dan of Dahomey and of Damballah of the West Indies, the god of Voodoo who also has a 'maidservant' who is a snake. Even old American Indian tribes used snakes in magic rituals, just as some modern Christian sects in the US handle snakes, claiming that their faith protects them.

54. Automatism, psychologists say, produces manifestations of layers of personality that are subconscious and have no link with the conscious mind. Hence, Sonuttara would have had no control over what he had to do.

55. The bringing into rhythm the life current with controlled breathing. This is then considered to become identical to the thought current, and forms the basis of all yoga techniques.

56. Hereward Carrington: *The Story of Psychic Science*, London, 1930.

57. This supernormal faculty is one of the six that monks, far along the path of Buddhistic wisdom, possess. In his *Dialogues of the Buddha*, Rhys Davids says these six powers or *Abhinna*, are *Iddhi*—the Heavenly Ear (or clairaudience); the power to read minds; the knowledge of former existences; the Heavenly Eye (or clairvoyance); and the abandonment of all desires.

58. Annie Besant: *Thought Forms*, Buddhist Theosophical Society, 1969; and Nandor Fedor: *Encyclopaedia of Psychic Science*, London, 1934.

59. In modern times, Professor Charles Richet has described this sensibility as a perception of things that include all phenonema, such as clairvoyance, premonition, psychometry, telepathy, etc., and is only possible through the intervention of spirits of past lives as well. He had termed this Cryptesthesia. What the astral body is charged with has been termed Faculty X by Colin Wilson in his book *The Occult*, London, 1971. According to Wilson, this power covers the latent power

that all human mind can reach, to go beyond the present to other realities of time and place. It is also the power to unite both sections of the mind—the conscious and the subconscious.

60. The trance state.

61. T. Bernard: *Hatha Yoga*, London, 1950. There are four Hatha yoga stages which enable an adept to 'get whatever he desires': *Pratyahara*— the withdrawing of the mind from all objects to which mind and body are drawn; *Dharana*—the development of concentration; *Dhyana*—meditation; and finally the trance state.

The Princess-Elect

62. As told in *Children of the Lion*.

63. Also Vihambija—a village to the south of Anuradhapura.

64. J.H. Hutton: *Caste in India: Its Native Function and Origins*, Cambridge, 1946.

65. Richard Fick: *The Social Organisation in North-East India in Buddha's Time*, S. Maitra (tr.), Calcutta, 1920.

66. E.H. Hare: *Woven Cadences of Early Buddhism*, London, 1944.

67. Bruce Ryan: *Caste in Modern Ceylon*, New Delhi, 1993.

68. B.C. Law: *India as Described in Early Texts of Buddhism and Jainism*, London, 1941.

69. This king became a devout Buddhist and endowed many lands for temples. He also encouraged Buddhist missionary activity between Lanka, Burma and Thailand. (See also, Brendon Gooneratne: *The Epic Struggle of the Kingdom of Kandy*, 'The Sally Sage and David McAlpine lecture', 1990, London, 1995.)

70. R.S. Copleston: *Buddhism—Primitive and Present in Magadha and in Ceylon*, London, 1892.

71. The Buddhist law of causation and the doctrine of rebirth.

72. The final spiritual attainment and the cessation of rebirth.

73. The caste of nobles and kings.

Kingly Acceptance

74. *Dipavamsa,* I.24 and V.4.

75. The thera Maha Kassapa, who took it on himself to establish the holy truth and make a compilation of the Dhamma. As the *Mahavamsa* says, 'The thera Maha Kassapa has made the Blessed Buddha's message to endure five hundred years.'

76. *Culavagga: The Vinaya Pitaka,* H. Oldenberg (ed.), Vol. II, 1880.

77. A place not far from Takkshila in Western India.

78. One can read of the confederacy of the Vajji in Rhys Davids: *Buddhist India.* According to V. Smith: *Early History of India,* and the *Journal of the Royal Asiatic Society,* 1902, the Vajjis of Vesali were concentrated in the Muzaffarpur district north of Patna in what is today known as Basar.

79. Also known as Kusumapura.

80. J.F. Fleet: Article in the *Journal of the Royal Asiatic Society,* 1910.

81. This is given by Beal in the journal *Indian Antiquarian,* 1910.

82. Old texts also refer to him as Aravada.

83. This story is preserved in the Chinese Vinaya with an English translation by J. Vogel: *Indian Serpent Lore,* also reproduced in the *Journal Asiatique,* 1914, and incorporated in the *Vinaya Atthakatha,* J. Takasukusu and M. Nagai (eds), Pali Text Society, 1924–47. It is also told of by J.N & P.N. Gankar: *Buddhism in Kashmir and Ladakh.*

84. This is told of in *Children of the Lion.*

85. This is the name of the mythical Mount Meru which is the central point of the universe.

86. The *Mahavamsa* adds that the ring of his body was 300 yojanas long and one yojana was his measure around. Turnour's translation gives the serpent's hood as forty yojanas broad, but this is not mentioned in the text.

87. The four holy truth of Buddhism. These form the foundation of the Buddhist doctrine: truths concerning sorrow, the cause of sorrow, the cessation of sorrow, and the way leading to the cessation of sorrow. It would be opportune, at this moment, to ask why temples, churches, cathedrals and other places of worship and religious devotion seem to find it necessary, to this day, to fill their chambers with precious stuff, works of art and costly trappings. It has always been asked whether these are for the exhaltation of the gods or the exhaltation of the priests who are surely corrupted by the great wealth they surround themselves with.

88. Timbaru is also called Gandhabba Raja and is honoured by actors, players and dancers.

89. These are the four cardinal points, and the north-east.

90. The Asoka monastery in the capital, Pataliputta.

91. A sutta called the *Sariputra* specifies the exact proportions to be used when scaling a Buddha image. 'Sariputra' means 'Instructions to Image Makers' and while it dates to the fifth century AD it is obviously the result of long years of oral tradition. Perhaps this accounts for why so many images, thousands of miles apart, look exactly alike in whatever position they are made. Among other things, the *Sariputra* prescribes the following: That the height of the face shall be the height of three noses with the nose in the centre; the neck shall be the same length as the hair from eyeline to crown; the length, standing or reclining, shall be the length of nine faces; the trunk shall be the length of three faces;

Carl Muller

the thigh and shank shall each be three faces. In Sri Lanka, the instructions of the *Sariputra* were used rigorously, but later there were embellishments added based on ancestral, local deities, Hindu gods, etc.

92. The *Lakhana Suttanta* in the *Dighaya Nikaya* gives a full listing and description of these signs.

Enshrinement And The Road To Immortality

93. Silver Temple.

94. A hot and wet region lying west of the Central Province.

95. The *vadu riyana.*

96. *Pada.*

97. *Viyata.*

98. Also vadu angala—presumably an inch, but accepted as the distance from first to second joint of the forefinger.

99. Ananda Coomaraswamy: *Medieval Sinhalese Art,* New York, 1956.

100. Face.

101. Very small.

102. Small.

103. Middling.

104. Large.

105. Very large or great.

106. The protuberance upon the skull which is one of the thirty-two great signs of the Buddha.

107. One-eighth of an inch or a barleycorn.

108. May, or June–July.

109. The Buddhist Sabbath, considered a holy day for monks and laymen, occurring four times in the month—on full moon and new moon days and on the eighth day following the full and new moon. The Sanskrit term is *upavasatha.*

110. This is the Chant of the Great Victory.

111. The Jewels Chant.

112. Readers will recall that these two samaneras brought the massive fat-coloured stones for the main chamber from the land of the Kurus.

113. The square capital which would form the base for the conical spire. This is generally known by the Burmese term, *tee*. The conical spire or chatta crowns the whole. As the *Mahavamsa* says, sometimes a sort of roof or temple was built over the tope.

Past Life, Future Merit

114. After his enlightenment, the Buddha, after a certain time spent in close proximity to the Bodhi tree, went to the Deer Park where he preached his first sermon—the setting into the motion of the Wheel of the Dhamma. Seven events during these seven weeks are now popular Buddhist lore and the subject of many image house paintings to this day.

115. The *Vessantara Jataka* was painted in detail. This describes the Buddha's life in the last incarnation and, in Sri Lanka, it is often repeated through the night by the bereaved, just before a dead member of the household is taken for cremation on the following day. Vessantara, the king of that day, came to realize that earthly riches only had any real significance if they were given away. The more one seeks to posssess them, the less is one satisfied; the more one gives them up, the more they fall into one's hands. Vessantara gave up his kingdom, his armies, his treasury, his horse. He then gave up his wife, children, his garments and finally himself. Thus, he gained everything. This Jataka is one of the great treasures of Lankan Buddhist Literature. It has hundreds of stanzas.

116. Chief disciples of the Buddha.

117. In the Central Province of Sri Lanka, some families still hold some of these original templates which were much in use during the Kandyan kingdom's renaissance of Buddhist art in the eighteenth century.

118. It is believed to have been either of pork or of mushrooms.

119. Cycads.

120. Indian laburnum—*Cassia fistula.*

121. *Tampani* in Tamil—*Mischodon zeylanica.*

122. The *Mahavamsa* says that in all, there were 96 kotis of bhikkhus.

123. The Panjali Mountain or Pabbata is near the source of the Kirinda River or Magama Ganga, five miles north of Wellawaya and east of Hambantota on Lanka's east coast. The river's source is in the mountains south of Badulla. It is on this mountain that the Kande Vihara was built, believed to trace back to Duttha Gamani's father, Kakavana Tissa.

124. The story of Duttha Gamani's former existence is told in *Children of the Lion,* Chapter 32, 'Her Majesty's Service'.

125. See Chapter 5, 'The Flowing of the Favourable Flood' in *Children of the Lion.*

Illusion And Delusion

126. Artisans and those engaged in personal service.

127. Tailors. These men belonged to the Kshruda caste. It was also believed that the immense quantity of white cotton cloth was first washed by the people of the Durawo caste—the Paliyo or Apullana—the washermen.

128. The weavers and plaiters of reeds.

129. Obviously, Tissa needed to make the mock spire to look as real as possible in texture and colour. Kankutthaka is a kind of silvery-coloured mould.

130. Painters.

131. Gold and silversmiths.

132. The *Mahavamsa* calls this the *Pancangulikapantika*. It is not clear what sort of ornaments these were.

133. *Terminalia bellerica.*

134. The Buddhist full-moon festival celebrating the Buddha's victory over death, or nibbana, which falls in March–April.

135. Steamed cakes. Sanskrit: *Jalapuva.*

136. This is a sermon of the Buddha, and is found in the *Sutta Nipata,* ed. Fausboll.

137. This is thought to be about three pints of wine measure. Also known as *naliya.*

138. Adam's Peak.

139. The Kelani Vihara today, in Kelaniya, where the Kelani River flows past in its journey to the sea.

140. Panicum or Saffron Island, where monks of great holiness lived. Also called Piyaguka and Puvangu, and known as Pungudutivu today, in the far north-west of Sri Lanka.

141. It is not easy to establish where, in the southern kingdom, this village was, but the Sinhalese believe in the existence of a Talaguru Vihara in Ruhuna.

142. Known as the Mangana Vihara, in the north of Sri Lanka.

143. As far as is known, the Kesala Vihara was a monastery in India. It will be remembered that at the commencement of the work on the Maha Thupa, the thera Suriyagutta came from the Kesala Vihara with 96,000 monks.

144. A space marked off and usually terraced, within which holy ceremonies are observed. The Maha Vihara had thirty-two such malakas. In Anuradhapura today, the sacred Bo tree is surrounded by a malaka.

Peace...And The End Of Peace

145. This name has its variants: Lajji Tissa and Lanji Tissa.

146. The groud laid with slabs.

147. Parker called it *Hatthipakara* in *Ancient Ceylon*. The sustaining wall of the terrace on which the thupa stands also has similar figures of elephants in relief. In *Anuradhapura*, Smither thinks that this is of later origin.

148. B.W. Harischandra: *The Sacred City of Anuradhapura*, Colombo, 1908.

149. Pool of dark water.

150. Also Duratissa.

151. Dighavapi is in the Eastern Province, about 30 miles south-south-west of Batticaloa. In *Ancient Ceylon*, Parker refers to a large dagaba built there in the neighbourhood of the *vapi* or tank. This Dighavapi tank is also called Kandiya-kayyu. The Buddha's visit to Dighavapi is told of in the *Mahavamsa*—the third visit during which he is said to have visited Kelaniya, Adam's Peak, Dighavapi and Anuradhapura.

152. Also called Alakandara, Lakandara, Lokandara and Lokantara.

153. A.M. Hocart: 'Duplication of Office in Indian State: [A] The Two Queens', *Ceylon Journal of Science*, Setion G.1.

154. The head of the army.

155. The chief scribe.

156. The region west of the central mountains, as far as the sea coast, was the Dakkinadesa and only second in economic and political importance to the Rajarata—the kingdom of Anuradhapura. Lanja Tissa had extended his power to the western seaboard too, and held the entire east, south and west. That he used the term dakkhinadesa was significant, for it was always the custom of bestowing the dakkinadesa—the Southern Province—the rightful heir.

Lessons Unlearned

157. Anuradha Seneviratna: *Ancient Anuradhapura*, Colombo, 1994. In this work is given, on page 82, a plan of the monastic

city of Anuradhapura, showing how the layout, in squares, preserved a distinct order.

158. Literally, Inner City.

159. This was the only religious edifice within the citadel since the relic was a royal palladium. Where the relic lay, did the king reign, and it became vital to kingship to safeguard the Sacred Tooth. This is why, in later years, with the shifting of the kingdom, temples to hold the relic were raised wherever the king set up his throne. Somehow, with the end of kingship in Kandy, the relic has remained in the central capital and has not been moved since. This has contributed to the oft-spoken comment that with the government of the country based in Colombo and the relic remaining in Kandy, there is no real protection for present-day rulers. Concerned citizens have time and again insisted that the relic be housed in Colombo, where the government is, but this has been regarded in poor light by the relic's custodians. Yet, there is some feeling that the many ills that face the country today is due to the fact that the relic is not where the rulers are.

160. Also known as the Basavakkulama.

161. Also called the Isurumini.

162. Also called the Puliyankulama.

163. Also called the Pankuliya.

164. Also called the Kiribat Vihara. 'Uttara' means north.

165. The street that runs to the river.

166. Polonnaruwa today.

A Cauldron Of Kings

167. Ananda K. Coomaraswamy: *The Dance of Shiva* and *Hinduism and Buddhism.*

168. Professor Radhakrishnan: *Gautama the Buddha.*

Carl Muller

169. H.W. Codrington: *'Ancient Land Tenure and Revenue in Ceylon'*, Colombo, 1938.

170. Nigamas are mentioned in the Badulla pillar inscription, *Epigraphia Zeylanica,* Vol. 3, and the Polonnaruwa Hatadage Vestibule wall inscription, *Epigraphia Zeylanica,* Vol. 2.

171. Mantai.

172. Trincomalee.

173. *Upasakaganalankaraya,* ed. Sugunupala Thera.

174. D.T. Devendra: *Tanks and Rice,* Colombo, 1965.

175. The Thuparama is 400 yards north of the Ruvanweliseya.

176. The six garments: the *Mahavamsa* tells us that Lanja Tissa distributed the six garments each to 60,000 bhikkhus. What each monk received was a pair of each of the three articles of clothig called the *ticivara.* They are the *ataravasaka* (shirt to serve as an undergarment), the *uttarasanga* (robe) and the *samghati* (mantle).

177. The Malwatta River.

178. It would be interesting to consider such Buddhist discourses as the *Sakkapanna Sutra,* and also S.D. Lanerolle's *Origins of Sinhala Culture.* In the *Sakkapanna Sutra,* there is evidence that the god Sakka and his devas were human beings. Lanerolle says: 'Having heard that Sakka has come to ask questions from the Buddha, Mahali, King of the Lichchavis, came to the Buddha to find out if it were true that Sakka had visited him. Mahali inquired from the Buddha if it was not somebody else in the guise of Sakka that came to see him. Then the Buddha replied that it was not so, that it was the Sakka himself who had come and that he knew Sakka personally and, what was more, he was aware of all the attributes that raised him to that exalted position. This little dialogue doesn't give the impression that Mahali and the Buddha were talking about a non-human. If there was a belief in Buddha's time of a Sakka who could be invisible and also vanish into thin air, there was no need

for Mahali to ask such a question, nor the Buddha to give such a reply.' Scholars today believe that Sakka was indeed the Persian emperor Darius. It is known that the Persian Empire extended up to the Indus and its influence even further south. The Sakyas of India also gave their support to Darius. Darius also erected the Behistan stone inscription in which is recorded that he belonged to the royal dynasty of Hakka or Sakka...meaning the solar disc or wheel that was the symbol of royalty, as well as of the supreme deity. It is also said that in the seventh year after his enlightenment, the Buddha spent three months in the palace of Sakka and of how Sakka created a golden ladder for the Buddha to descend from his palace. This has been taken to claim that Sakka's palace was in the skies, hence the need for the golden ladder. This is the most simplistic way texts have been interpreted to keep the aura of the supernatural. In truth, Buddha was in Darius's gorgeous palace at Persepolis, where the main attraction was the magnificent stairway leading to the *Apadana*—Audience Hall. There is no doubt, if the visit to Persepolis is believed, that the Buddha stepped down this 'golden stairway'—and the Chinese traveller and bhikkhu, Hiuen-Tsang, tells of how he saw a model of this ladder or staircase in India. Many of Sri Lanka's temples also display paintings of this ladder. It is also significant that Buddhist architecture lays emphasis on flights of steps flanked by ornate balustrades, guard stones and moonstones. It is also ancient tradition to call people by the name of their cult and their dynastic names. Hence, the serpent worshippers were nagas, the demon worshippers yakshas, and god worshippers devas. The Buddha also referred to Darius by his dynastic name, Sakka. This would explain why Lanka has no shrine for the worship of devas. Buddhism, on coming to the island, must have accepted that these devas were human. Sadly, in later years, Buddhism was engulfed by the myths and mystic cult forms of India's theistic religions and their worship of devas became part and parcel of the faith.

179. A king-father.
180. Near Polonnaruwa.
181. Eight miles south of Polonnaruwa.
182. On the eastern side of the Mahaweli River. Also called Dolapabbata, Dolangapabbata or Dolagala.
183. Mantota—Mannar today.
184. Also Kolombahalaka, situated not far from the north gate of the city.
185. Jaina ascetic who went about naked.
186. This relic was brought to Lanka by the samanera, Sumana, during the reign of King Devanampiyatissa (247–207 BC).
187. South of Vessagiriya.
188. In the hill country.